50 Sweet Treats without Sugar Recipes for Home

By: Kelly Johnson

Table of Contents

- Chocolate Avocado Mousse
- Almond Butter Cookies
- Berry Coconut Chia Pudding
- Date-Sweetened Brownies
- Peanut Butter Energy Balls
- Coconut Macaroons
- Apple Cinnamon Oat Bars
- Frozen Banana Bites
- Pumpkin Spice Muffins
- Raspberry Lemon Bars
- Caramelized Banana Sundae
- Nutty Chocolate Bark
- Greek Yogurt Parfait with Berries
- Coconut Cream Pie
- Sweet Potato Brownies
- Maple Pecan Granola
- Cinnamon Roasted Almonds
- Chia Seed Strawberry Jam
- Raw Chocolate Protein Balls
- Homemade Fruit Sorbet
- Coconut-Almond Truffles
- Apple Nachos with Almond Butter
- Berry-Packed Crumble
- Coconut-Date Energy Bars
- Frozen Fruit Bars
- Baked Cinnamon Apples
- Avocado Lime Cheesecake
- Almond Flour Pancakes
- Peach Coconut Muffins
- Walnut Date Balls
- Carrot Cake Bites
- Berry Coconut Popsicles
- Cashew Butter Brownies
- Coconut Lime Energy Balls
- Baked Banana Chips
- Zucchini Brownies

- Almond Joy Energy Bites
- Raspberry Coconut Bars
- Apple-Pear Crumble
- Strawberry Banana Ice Cream
- Chocolate-Dipped Strawberries
- Nutty Fig Bars
- Blueberry Almond Muffins
- Pineapple Coconut Cake
- Peanut Butter Cup Muffins
- Spiced Pumpkin Energy Balls
- Gingerbread Date Bars
- Frozen Yogurt Bark
- Coconut Raspberry Muffins
- Chocolate Chia Seed Pudding

Chocolate Avocado Mousse

Ingredients:

- **2 ripe avocados** (peeled, pitted, and chopped)
- **1/4 cup cocoa powder** (unsweetened)
- **1/4 cup pure maple syrup** (or honey, agave syrup, or another liquid sweetener of your choice)
- **1/4 cup coconut milk** (or any milk of your choice)
- **1 teaspoon vanilla extract**
- **Pinch of salt**
- **Optional toppings:** Fresh berries, shredded coconut, chopped nuts, or a dollop of whipped coconut cream

Instructions:

1. **Blend the Ingredients:**
     - In a food processor or blender, combine the avocados, cocoa powder, maple syrup, coconut milk, vanilla extract, and a pinch of salt.
     - Blend until smooth and creamy, scraping down the sides as needed to ensure everything is well incorporated.
2. **Taste and Adjust:**
     - Taste the mousse and adjust sweetness or cocoa powder as needed, blending again if you make any changes.
3. **Chill the Mousse:**
     - Transfer the mousse to serving dishes or bowls.
     - Refrigerate for at least 30 minutes to allow it to set and chill. This also helps to enhance the flavors.
4. **Serve:**
     - Before serving, top with your choice of optional toppings such as fresh berries, shredded coconut, or chopped nuts.
5. **Enjoy:**
     - Serve chilled and enjoy your creamy, chocolatey, guilt-free dessert!

Tips:

- **Texture:** If the mousse is too thick, you can add a bit more coconut milk to reach your desired consistency.
- **Sweetness:** Adjust the sweetness to your taste. Some people may prefer a bit more maple syrup or honey, depending on their preference for sweetness.

This chocolate avocado mousse is a deliciously healthy dessert option that's rich in flavor and full of healthy fats from the avocado. Enjoy!

Almond Butter Cookies

Ingredients:

- **1 cup almond butter** (smooth or crunchy, preferably unsweetened)
- **1/2 cup honey** or **pure maple syrup** (for a refined sugar-free option)
- **1 large egg**
- **1 teaspoon vanilla extract**
- **1/2 teaspoon baking soda**
- **1/4 teaspoon salt**
- **Optional mix-ins:** Chocolate chips, chopped nuts, or dried fruit (about 1/2 cup total)

Instructions:

1. **Preheat Oven:**
    - Preheat your oven to 350°F (175°C).
    - Line a baking sheet with parchment paper or a silicone baking mat.
2. **Mix Ingredients:**
    - In a medium bowl, combine the almond butter, honey (or maple syrup), egg, and vanilla extract.
    - Stir until well combined.
3. **Add Dry Ingredients:**
    - Add the baking soda and salt to the almond butter mixture.
    - Mix until fully incorporated.
4. **Incorporate Optional Mix-ins:**
    - If using chocolate chips, chopped nuts, or dried fruit, fold them into the dough now.
5. **Shape the Cookies:**
    - Scoop tablespoon-sized portions of dough and roll them into balls.
    - Place them on the prepared baking sheet, spacing them about 2 inches apart.
    - Flatten each ball slightly with the back of a fork or your fingers to form a cookie shape.
6. **Bake:**
    - Bake in the preheated oven for about 10-12 minutes, or until the edges are golden brown.
    - The cookies may seem soft when you take them out, but they will firm up as they cool.
7. **Cool:**
    - Allow the cookies to cool on the baking sheet for about 5 minutes before transferring them to a wire rack to cool completely.
8. **Serve:**
    - Enjoy your almond butter cookies with a glass of milk or as a standalone treat!

Tips:

- **Consistency:** Make sure your almond butter is well-stirred and not too runny or too thick. Natural almond butters may separate, so mix it well before using.
- **Storage:** Store the cookies in an airtight container at room temperature for up to a week, or freeze for longer storage.

These almond butter cookies are easy to make, satisfying, and a great option for those with dietary restrictions. Enjoy your homemade cookies!

Berry Coconut Chia Pudding

Ingredients:

- **1/4 cup chia seeds**
- **1 cup coconut milk** (canned or carton; for a richer pudding, use full-fat coconut milk)
- **1/4 cup maple syrup** or **honey** (adjust to taste)
- **1/2 teaspoon vanilla extract**
- **1 cup mixed berries** (fresh or frozen; such as strawberries, blueberries, raspberries)
- **Optional toppings:** Fresh mint, shredded coconut, nuts, or granola

Instructions:

1. **Prepare the Pudding:**
    - In a medium bowl, whisk together the chia seeds, coconut milk, maple syrup (or honey), and vanilla extract.
    - Let the mixture sit for about 5 minutes, then stir again to prevent clumping.
2. **Refrigerate:**
    - Cover the bowl and refrigerate for at least 2 hours, or overnight. The chia seeds will absorb the coconut milk and thicken into a pudding-like consistency.
3. **Prepare the Berries:**
    - If using frozen berries, thaw them slightly and mash them lightly with a fork or spoon to release their juices. If using fresh berries, you can also lightly mash them if desired.
4. **Assemble:**
    - Once the chia pudding has thickened, stir it to ensure it's well mixed.
    - Spoon the chia pudding into serving dishes or bowls.
5. **Top and Serve:**
    - Top with mixed berries and any optional toppings you like, such as fresh mint, shredded coconut, nuts, or granola.
6. **Enjoy:**
    - Serve immediately, or store in the refrigerator for up to 3 days.

Tips:

- **Adjust Sweetness:** You can adjust the sweetness by adding more or less maple syrup or honey according to your taste.
- **Consistency:** If the pudding is too thick after refrigeration, you can stir in a bit more coconut milk to reach your desired consistency.
- **Flavors:** Experiment with adding spices like cinnamon or cardamom, or a splash of lemon or orange juice for a different flavor profile.

Berry coconut chia pudding is not only a tasty treat but also a healthy option that's easy to prepare. Enjoy your creamy, fruity, and nutritious pudding!

Date-Sweetened Brownies

Ingredients:

- **1 cup pitted dates** (about 8-10 large dates)
- **1/2 cup water**
- **1/2 cup almond butter** (or other nut or seed butter)
- **1/4 cup unsweetened cocoa powder**
- **1/2 teaspoon vanilla extract**
- **1/4 teaspoon salt**
- **1/2 cup almond flour** (or all-purpose flour)
- **1/2 teaspoon baking powder**
- **Optional add-ins:** Chocolate chips, nuts, or dried fruit (about 1/2 cup total)

Instructions:

1. **Prepare the Dates:**
   - In a small saucepan, combine the pitted dates and water. Heat over medium heat until the dates are soft and the water is mostly absorbed, about 5-7 minutes.
   - Alternatively, you can soak the dates in hot water for about 10 minutes until soft.
2. **Blend the Date Mixture:**
   - Transfer the softened dates and any remaining water to a food processor or blender. Blend until smooth and creamy.
3. **Mix the Ingredients:**
   - In a large bowl, combine the date puree, almond butter, cocoa powder, vanilla extract, and salt. Mix until well combined.
   - Stir in the almond flour and baking powder until fully incorporated.
   - If using, fold in chocolate chips, nuts, or dried fruit.
4. **Prepare the Baking Pan:**
   - Preheat your oven to 350°F (175°C).
   - Line an 8x8-inch (20x20 cm) baking pan with parchment paper, or lightly grease the pan.
5. **Bake the Brownies:**
   - Spread the brownie batter evenly in the prepared baking pan.
   - Bake in the preheated oven for 20-25 minutes, or until a toothpick inserted into the center comes out with only a few moist crumbs.
6. **Cool and Slice:**
   - Allow the brownies to cool in the pan for about 10 minutes before transferring to a wire rack to cool completely.
   - Once cooled, cut into squares.
7. **Serve:**
   - Enjoy your date-sweetened brownies as a healthier dessert or snack!

Tips:

- **Date Prep:** Ensure the dates are very soft for a smooth batter. If they are a bit dry, you can soak them in hot water for a few minutes before blending.
- **Texture:** These brownies are fudgy and may be a bit softer than traditional brownies. Let them cool completely to set properly.
- **Storage:** Store the brownies in an airtight container at room temperature for up to 5 days, or refrigerate for longer shelf life.

These date-sweetened brownies offer a rich, chocolatey flavor while using natural sweetness and healthy ingredients. Enjoy!

Peanut Butter Energy Balls

Ingredients:

- **1 cup natural peanut butter** (creamy or crunchy)
- **1 cup old-fashioned oats** (uncooked)
- **1/2 cup honey** or **pure maple syrup** (for a refined sugar-free option)
- **1/2 cup ground flaxseed** (optional, for added nutrition)
- **1/4 cup mini chocolate chips** or **cocoa nibs** (optional)
- **1/4 cup chia seeds** (optional, for extra texture and nutrients)
- **1 teaspoon vanilla extract**
- **Pinch of salt** (optional, to taste)

Instructions:

1. **Mix Ingredients:**
   - In a large bowl, combine the peanut butter, oats, honey (or maple syrup), and vanilla extract.
   - Stir until well combined.
2. **Add Optional Ingredients:**
   - If using, mix in the ground flaxseed, chocolate chips, chia seeds, and a pinch of salt.
   - Stir until the mixture is evenly distributed.
3. **Form the Balls:**
   - Scoop out small amounts of the mixture (about 1 tablespoon each) and roll them into balls using your hands.
   - Place the balls on a parchment-lined baking sheet or plate.
4. **Chill:**
   - Refrigerate the energy balls for at least 30 minutes to firm up.
5. **Store:**
   - Store in an airtight container in the refrigerator for up to a week, or freeze for longer storage.
6. **Enjoy:**
   - Enjoy these peanut butter energy balls as a quick snack or a pre-workout boost!

Tips:

- **Consistency:** If the mixture is too dry and difficult to roll into balls, you can add a little more peanut butter or honey to moisten it.
- **Mix-ins:** Feel free to experiment with other mix-ins such as dried fruit, shredded coconut, or nuts to vary the flavor and texture.
- **Sweetness:** Adjust the sweetness by adding more honey or maple syrup if desired.

Peanut butter energy balls are a convenient and satisfying snack that combines the rich taste of peanut butter with the nutritional benefits of oats and optional add-ins. Enjoy your homemade energy balls!

Coconut Macaroons

Ingredients:

- **2 1/2 cups sweetened shredded coconut**
- **1/2 cup granulated sugar** (or coconut sugar for a less refined option)
- **1/4 cup all-purpose flour** (or almond flour for a gluten-free option)
- **1/4 teaspoon salt**
- **3 large egg whites**
- **1 teaspoon vanilla extract**
- **Optional: 1/2 cup chocolate chips** or **melted chocolate** for dipping

Instructions:

1. **Preheat Oven:**
    - Preheat your oven to 325°F (165°C).
    - Line a baking sheet with parchment paper or a silicone baking mat.
2. **Prepare the Mixture:**
    - In a large bowl, combine the shredded coconut, sugar, flour (or almond flour), and salt. Mix well.
    - In a separate bowl, beat the egg whites until stiff peaks form (you can use an electric mixer for this).
    - Gently fold the beaten egg whites into the coconut mixture until fully combined.
    - Stir in the vanilla extract.
3. **Shape the Macaroons:**
    - Using a small cookie scoop or spoon, drop rounded tablespoons of the mixture onto the prepared baking sheet, spacing them about 1 inch apart.
    - Gently press down on each mound to help them hold their shape.
4. **Bake:**
    - Bake in the preheated oven for 15-20 minutes, or until the macaroons are golden brown on the edges.
    - Allow them to cool on the baking sheet for a few minutes before transferring them to a wire rack to cool completely.
5. **Optional: Chocolate Coating:**
    - If desired, dip the cooled macaroons in melted chocolate or drizzle melted chocolate over the top.
    - To melt the chocolate, heat it in a microwave-safe bowl in 20-second intervals, stirring between each interval, until fully melted and smooth.
6. **Store:**
    - Store macaroons in an airtight container at room temperature for up to a week, or in the refrigerator for a longer shelf life.

Tips:

- **Egg Whites:** Make sure there is no trace of yolk in the egg whites, as any fat can prevent them from whipping properly.
- **Shape:** For a more uniform shape, use a small cookie scoop or melon baller.
- **Variation:** You can add a pinch of almond extract or a few tablespoons of chopped nuts to the coconut mixture for extra flavor.

Coconut macaroons are a wonderfully sweet and chewy treat that's easy to make and perfect for any occasion. Enjoy your homemade macaroons!

Apple Cinnamon Oat Bars

Ingredients:

- **1 1/2 cups old-fashioned oats**
- **1 cup almond flour** (or all-purpose flour)
- **1/2 cup coconut sugar** or **brown sugar** (adjust to taste)
- **1 teaspoon ground cinnamon**
- **1/4 teaspoon salt**
- **1/2 teaspoon baking powder**
- **1/4 cup coconut oil** or **butter** (melted)
- **1 large egg**
- **1 teaspoon vanilla extract**
- **1 cup diced apples** (peeled, cored, and small-diced)
- **Optional: 1/4 cup chopped nuts** or **raisins**

Instructions:

1. **Preheat Oven:**
   - Preheat your oven to 350°F (175°C).
   - Line an 8x8-inch (20x20 cm) baking pan with parchment paper or lightly grease it.
2. **Prepare Dry Ingredients:**
   - In a large bowl, combine the oats, almond flour (or all-purpose flour), coconut sugar, ground cinnamon, salt, and baking powder. Mix well.
3. **Prepare Wet Ingredients:**
   - In another bowl, whisk together the melted coconut oil (or butter), egg, and vanilla extract.
4. **Combine Ingredients:**
   - Pour the wet ingredients into the dry ingredients and mix until just combined.
   - Fold in the diced apples and optional nuts or raisins.
5. **Spread and Bake:**
   - Spread the mixture evenly in the prepared baking pan, pressing it down firmly with a spatula.
   - Bake in the preheated oven for 25-30 minutes, or until the edges are golden brown and a toothpick inserted into the center comes out clean.
6. **Cool and Slice:**
   - Allow the bars to cool in the pan for about 10 minutes before transferring to a wire rack to cool completely.
   - Once completely cool, cut into squares or rectangles.
7. **Serve:**
   - Enjoy your apple cinnamon oat bars as a snack, breakfast, or a wholesome treat!

Tips:

- **Apples:** Use firm apples like Honeycrisp, Fuji, or Granny Smith for the best texture. Avoid using overly juicy apples as they might make the bars too moist.
- **Texture:** For a chewier texture, you can use extra old-fashioned oats. For a slightly softer bar, use quick oats.
- **Storage:** Store the oat bars in an airtight container at room temperature for up to a week or in the refrigerator for longer freshness. They can also be frozen for up to 3 months.

These apple cinnamon oat bars are a great way to enjoy the flavors of fall year-round with minimal effort. Enjoy!

Frozen Banana Bites

Ingredients:

- **2 ripe bananas**
- **1/4 cup almond butter** (or peanut butter, or any nut/seed butter of your choice)
- **1/4 cup chocolate chips** (optional)
- **1 tablespoon coconut oil** (for melting chocolate, optional)
- **Optional toppings:** Shredded coconut, crushed nuts, sprinkles, or sea salt

Instructions:

1. **Prepare the Bananas:**
   - Peel the bananas and slice them into bite-sized pieces (about 1/2-inch thick).
2. **Prepare the Nut Butter:**
   - If using almond butter or peanut butter, you can warm it slightly to make it easier to spread. This can be done by microwaving it in a small bowl for 10-15 seconds.
3. **Coat the Banana Slices:**
   - Spread a small amount of nut butter on one side of each banana slice.
   - Press another banana slice on top to create a "sandwich."
4. **Optional: Coat with Chocolate:**
   - If you want to add a chocolate coating, melt the chocolate chips with coconut oil in a microwave-safe bowl. Heat in 20-second intervals, stirring between each interval until smooth.
   - Dip each banana sandwich into the melted chocolate, covering half or the entire piece. Use a fork or toothpick to help with dipping and draining off excess chocolate.
5. **Add Toppings:**
   - If desired, sprinkle the banana bites with optional toppings like shredded coconut, crushed nuts, sprinkles, or a pinch of sea salt before the chocolate sets.
6. **Freeze:**
   - Place the banana bites on a parchment-lined baking sheet or plate.
   - Freeze for at least 1-2 hours, or until the banana bites are solid.
7. **Serve:**
   - Enjoy the frozen banana bites straight from the freezer. They make a refreshing and healthy treat!

Tips:

- **Texture:** For a slightly softer texture, you can freeze the banana bites for a shorter time, but they will be less firm.
- **Chocolate Variations:** You can use dark chocolate, milk chocolate, or white chocolate depending on your preference.
- **Storage:** Store leftover banana bites in an airtight container in the freezer for up to 3 months.

Frozen banana bites are a fun, customizable treat that's both delicious and nutritious. Enjoy your homemade frozen goodies!

Pumpkin Spice Muffins

Ingredients:

- **1 1/2 cups all-purpose flour** (or whole wheat flour for a healthier option)
- **1 cup canned pumpkin** (pure pumpkin puree, not pumpkin pie filling)
- **1/2 cup granulated sugar** (or coconut sugar)
- **1/4 cup brown sugar** (packed)
- **1/2 cup vegetable oil** (or melted coconut oil)
- **2 large eggs**
- **1/2 cup milk** (dairy or non-dairy, such as almond or oat milk)
- **1 teaspoon vanilla extract**
- **1 teaspoon ground cinnamon**
- **1/2 teaspoon ground nutmeg**
- **1/4 teaspoon ground cloves**
- **1/2 teaspoon baking soda**
- **1 1/2 teaspoons baking powder**
- **1/4 teaspoon salt**
- **Optional: 1/2 cup chopped nuts** (such as walnuts or pecans) or **1/4 cup chocolate chips**

Instructions:

1. **Preheat Oven:**
   - Preheat your oven to 350°F (175°C).
   - Line a 12-cup muffin tin with paper liners or lightly grease it.
2. **Prepare Dry Ingredients:**
   - In a medium bowl, whisk together the flour, baking soda, baking powder, salt, cinnamon, nutmeg, and cloves. Set aside.
3. **Prepare Wet Ingredients:**
   - In a large bowl, whisk together the pumpkin puree, granulated sugar, brown sugar, vegetable oil, eggs, milk, and vanilla extract until smooth and well combined.
4. **Combine Ingredients:**
   - Gradually add the dry ingredients to the wet ingredients, mixing just until combined. Be careful not to overmix.
   - If using, fold in the chopped nuts or chocolate chips.
5. **Fill Muffin Tin:**
   - Divide the batter evenly among the 12 muffin cups, filling each about 2/3 full.
6. **Bake:**
   - Bake in the preheated oven for 18-22 minutes, or until a toothpick inserted into the center of a muffin comes out clean.
7. **Cool:**
   - Allow the muffins to cool in the tin for about 5 minutes before transferring them to a wire rack to cool completely.

8. **Serve:**
    - Enjoy your pumpkin spice muffins warm or at room temperature. They are perfect on their own or with a spread of butter or cream cheese.

Tips:

- **Texture:** For a lighter muffin, you can use a combination of all-purpose flour and whole wheat flour, or try using a gluten-free flour blend.
- **Spices:** Adjust the spices to your preference. If you like a stronger spice flavor, you can increase the amounts of cinnamon, nutmeg, and cloves.
- **Storage:** Store muffins in an airtight container at room temperature for up to 4 days. They can also be frozen for up to 3 months. To freeze, wrap each muffin individually in plastic wrap or foil and place them in a freezer-safe bag or container.

These pumpkin spice muffins are a delightful treat that captures the essence of fall with every bite. Enjoy baking and savoring them!

Raspberry Lemon Bars

Ingredients:

For the Crust:

- **1 1/2 cups all-purpose flour**
- **1/2 cup granulated sugar**
- **1/2 cup unsalted butter** (cold, cut into small pieces)
- **1/4 teaspoon salt**

For the Filling:

- **1 cup granulated sugar**
- **1/4 cup all-purpose flour**
- **4 large eggs**
- **1/2 cup freshly squeezed lemon juice** (about 2-3 lemons)
- **1 tablespoon lemon zest** (from about 1 lemon)
- **1/2 cup fresh raspberries** (or frozen, thawed and drained)
- **Powdered sugar** (for dusting, optional)

Instructions:

1. **Preheat Oven:**
    - Preheat your oven to 350°F (175°C).
    - Line an 8x8-inch (20x20 cm) baking pan with parchment paper, leaving an overhang on the sides for easy removal, or lightly grease the pan.
2. **Make the Crust:**
    - In a medium bowl, combine the flour, sugar, and salt.
    - Cut in the cold butter using a pastry cutter or your fingers until the mixture resembles coarse crumbs.
    - Press the mixture evenly into the bottom of the prepared baking pan.
3. **Bake the Crust:**
    - Bake in the preheated oven for 15-18 minutes, or until lightly golden brown. Remove from the oven and set aside.
4. **Prepare the Filling:**
    - In a medium bowl, whisk together the granulated sugar and flour.
    - Add the eggs and whisk until smooth.
    - Stir in the lemon juice and lemon zest until well combined.
5. **Add Raspberries:**
    - Gently fold in the fresh raspberries. Be careful not to break them up too much.
6. **Bake the Bars:**
    - Pour the lemon-raspberry filling over the pre-baked crust, spreading it evenly.
    - Bake in the oven for 25-30 minutes, or until the filling is set and slightly firm to the touch. The edges should be lightly golden.

7. **Cool:**
   - Allow the bars to cool completely in the pan on a wire rack.
   - Once cooled, use the parchment paper overhang to lift the bars out of the pan.
8. **Dust and Slice:**
   - Dust the top with powdered sugar if desired.
   - Cut into squares or rectangles.
9. **Serve:**
   - Serve chilled or at room temperature. Enjoy your refreshing and tangy raspberry lemon bars!

Tips:

- **Lemon Juice:** Freshly squeezed lemon juice provides the best flavor, but bottled lemon juice can be used in a pinch.
- **Raspberries:** If using frozen raspberries, thaw and drain them to avoid excess moisture in the filling.
- **Storage:** Store the lemon bars in an airtight container in the refrigerator for up to a week. They can also be frozen for up to 3 months. To freeze, wrap each bar individually and place in a freezer-safe bag or container.

These raspberry lemon bars offer a delightful combination of sweet, tangy, and fruity flavors that are sure to please your taste buds. Enjoy!

Caramelized Banana Sundae

Ingredients:

For the Caramelized Bananas:

- **2 large ripe bananas** (peeled and sliced into 1/2-inch thick rounds)
- **2 tablespoons unsalted butter**
- **1/4 cup brown sugar** (packed)
- **1/2 teaspoon ground cinnamon** (optional)

For the Sundae:

- **Vanilla ice cream** (or your favorite flavor)
- **Whipped cream** (optional)
- **Chopped nuts** (such as pecans or walnuts, optional)
- **Chocolate sauce** or **caramel sauce** (for drizzling, optional)
- **Maraschino cherries** (for garnish, optional)

Instructions:

1. **Caramelize the Bananas:**
    - In a large skillet, melt the butter over medium heat.
    - Add the brown sugar and stir until it begins to dissolve and combine with the butter.
    - Add the banana slices to the skillet. Cook for about 2-3 minutes on each side, or until the bananas are golden brown and caramelized. Be careful not to overcook them, as they can become mushy.
    - Sprinkle the cinnamon over the bananas if using, and stir gently to combine. Remove from heat and set aside.
2. **Prepare the Sundae:**
    - Scoop your desired amount of vanilla ice cream into serving bowls or glasses.
    - Spoon the warm caramelized bananas over the ice cream.
3. **Add Toppings:**
    - Top with whipped cream if desired.
    - Drizzle with chocolate sauce or caramel sauce.
    - Sprinkle with chopped nuts for added crunch.
    - Garnish with a maraschino cherry if using.
4. **Serve:**
    - Serve immediately while the caramelized bananas are still warm and the ice cream is cold.

Tips:

- **Banana Ripeness:** Use ripe but not overly mushy bananas for the best texture and flavor when caramelizing.
- **Sauce:** You can use store-bought chocolate or caramel sauce, or make your own for a more personalized touch.
- **Serving:** For an extra touch of elegance, serve in sundae glasses or bowls and layer with additional toppings.

This caramelized banana sundae combines warm, sweet bananas with cool, creamy ice cream, creating a delightful contrast in flavors and textures. Enjoy this indulgent dessert!

Nutty Chocolate Bark

Ingredients:

- **12 ounces (340g) semi-sweet or dark chocolate chips** (or chopped chocolate)
- **1 cup mixed nuts** (such as almonds, walnuts, pecans, cashews, or hazelnuts, roughly chopped)
- **1/4 cup dried fruit** (such as cranberries, cherries, or raisins, optional)
- **1/4 teaspoon sea salt** (optional, for sprinkling)
- **1/4 cup white chocolate chips** (optional, for drizzling)

Instructions:

1. **Prepare the Pan:**
    - Line a baking sheet with parchment paper or a silicone baking mat. This will make it easier to remove the bark later.
2. **Melt the Chocolate:**
    - In a microwave-safe bowl, melt the chocolate in 20-30 second intervals, stirring between each interval until smooth and fully melted. Alternatively, you can melt the chocolate using a double boiler on the stovetop.
    - Be careful not to overheat the chocolate, as it can burn.
3. **Add Nuts and Optional Ingredients:**
    - Stir in the chopped nuts and dried fruit (if using) into the melted chocolate. Mix until well combined.
4. **Spread the Chocolate:**
    - Pour the chocolate mixture onto the prepared baking sheet and spread it into an even layer with a spatula.
5. **Add Toppings:**
    - Sprinkle additional nuts over the top of the chocolate.
    - If desired, sprinkle sea salt over the top for a touch of salty contrast.
    - For a decorative touch, melt the white chocolate chips and drizzle over the top of the chocolate bark. To melt the white chocolate, follow the same method as for the dark chocolate.
6. **Chill:**
    - Place the baking sheet in the refrigerator for about 1-2 hours, or until the chocolate is completely set and hardened.
7. **Break into Pieces:**
    - Once the chocolate is set, break it into pieces or shards.
8. **Serve and Store:**
    - Serve the nutty chocolate bark as a snack or gift it to friends and family.
    - Store in an airtight container at room temperature for up to 1-2 weeks, or in the refrigerator for longer freshness.

Tips:

- **Nuts:** Use your favorite nuts or a mix for different textures and flavors. Toasting the nuts lightly before adding them can enhance their flavor.
- **Add-Ins:** Feel free to experiment with other add-ins such as crushed pretzels, toffee bits, or mini marshmallows.
- **Chocolate:** Use high-quality chocolate for the best flavor. You can mix semi-sweet and dark chocolate for a richer taste.

Nutty chocolate bark is versatile and easy to customize, making it a perfect treat for any occasion. Enjoy making and sharing this delicious bark!

Greek Yogurt Parfait with Berries

Ingredients:

- **2 cups Greek yogurt** (plain or vanilla, or use dairy-free yogurt if preferred)
- **1 tablespoon honey** or **maple syrup** (optional, for sweetness)
- **1 cup fresh berries** (such as strawberries, blueberries, raspberries, or blackberries)
- **1/2 cup granola** (store-bought or homemade)
- **1/4 cup chopped nuts** (such as almonds, walnuts, or pecans, optional)
- **1 tablespoon chia seeds** (optional, for added texture and nutrients)
- **Fresh mint leaves** (optional, for garnish)

Instructions:

1. **Prepare the Yogurt:**
   - If using plain Greek yogurt and you prefer a sweeter taste, mix in the honey or maple syrup until well combined. If using vanilla yogurt, you can skip this step.
2. **Prepare the Berries:**
   - Wash and gently pat dry the berries. If using strawberries, hull and slice them into bite-sized pieces.
3. **Assemble the Parfait:**
   - In serving glasses or bowls, start by spooning a layer of Greek yogurt at the bottom.
   - Add a layer of fresh berries on top of the yogurt.
   - Sprinkle a layer of granola over the berries.
   - Repeat the layers until the glasses or bowls are filled. You can usually make 2-3 layers, depending on the size of your containers.
4. **Add Optional Toppings:**
   - Sprinkle chopped nuts and chia seeds on top for added texture and nutrition.
   - Garnish with fresh mint leaves if desired.
5. **Serve:**
   - Serve immediately or chill in the refrigerator for up to an hour before serving to let the flavors meld.

Tips:

- **Customization:** Feel free to customize the parfait with different fruits, such as mango, kiwi, or peaches. You can also use frozen berries if fresh ones are not available.
- **Granola:** Choose a granola with low added sugar or make your own for a healthier option. Homemade granola can be easily made with oats, nuts, seeds, and a touch of honey or maple syrup.
- **Texture:** For a creamier texture, you can use full-fat Greek yogurt. For a lighter option, opt for low-fat or non-fat Greek yogurt.
- **Storage:** If preparing in advance, keep the yogurt and granola separate until serving to prevent the granola from becoming soggy.

This Greek yogurt parfait with berries is a versatile and nutritious option that's both satisfying and easy to prepare. Enjoy your healthy and delicious parfait!

Coconut Cream Pie

Ingredients:

For the Pie Crust:

- **1 1/2 cups graham cracker crumbs** (about 12-14 graham crackers, crushed)
- **1/4 cup granulated sugar**
- **6 tablespoons unsalted butter** (melted)

For the Coconut Cream Filling:

- **1 can (13.5 ounces) full-fat coconut milk** (or use 1 cup coconut cream)
- **1 cup whole milk**
- **3/4 cup granulated sugar**
- **1/4 cup cornstarch**
- **1/4 teaspoon salt**
- **3 large egg yolks**
- **1 teaspoon vanilla extract**
- **1 cup sweetened shredded coconut**

For the Topping:

- **1 cup heavy whipping cream**
- **2 tablespoons powdered sugar**
- **1/2 teaspoon vanilla extract**
- **1/4 cup toasted coconut flakes** (for garnish)

Instructions:

1. **Prepare the Pie Crust:**
   - Preheat your oven to 350°F (175°C).
   - In a medium bowl, combine the graham cracker crumbs, granulated sugar, and melted butter. Mix until the crumbs are evenly coated and resemble wet sand.
   - Press the mixture firmly into the bottom and up the sides of a 9-inch pie dish.
   - Bake the crust for 8-10 minutes, or until golden brown. Remove from the oven and let it cool completely.
2. **Make the Coconut Cream Filling:**
   - In a medium saucepan, whisk together the coconut milk, whole milk, sugar, cornstarch, and salt. Cook over medium heat, whisking constantly until the mixture starts to thicken and comes to a gentle boil.
   - In a small bowl, whisk the egg yolks. Slowly pour a small amount of the hot milk mixture into the egg yolks while whisking to temper them.
   - Pour the tempered egg yolks back into the saucepan and continue to cook for another 2-3 minutes, whisking constantly, until the filling is thickened and smooth.
   - Remove from heat and stir in the vanilla extract and shredded coconut.

- Let the filling cool slightly before pouring it into the prepared pie crust.
3. **Chill the Pie:**
    - Refrigerate the pie for at least 4 hours, or until the filling is set and firm.
4. **Prepare the Topping:**
    - In a medium bowl, beat the heavy cream, powdered sugar, and vanilla extract until stiff peaks form.
    - Spread or pipe the whipped cream over the chilled pie.
5. **Garnish:**
    - Sprinkle the toasted coconut flakes over the top of the whipped cream for added texture and flavor.
6. **Serve:**
    - Slice and serve the pie chilled. Enjoy!

Tips:

- **Toasted Coconut:** To toast coconut flakes, spread them in a single layer on a baking sheet and bake at 350°F (175°C) for 5-7 minutes, stirring occasionally, until golden brown.
- **Texture:** For a richer pie, use coconut cream instead of coconut milk. You can also add extra coconut extract for a more intense coconut flavor.
- **Storage:** Store the pie in the refrigerator for up to 3-4 days. It can also be frozen for longer storage; just make sure to wrap it well and thaw it in the refrigerator before serving.

Coconut cream pie is a creamy, dreamy dessert that's perfect for any occasion, bringing a taste of tropical paradise to your table. Enjoy!

Sweet Potato Brownies

Ingredients:

- **1 medium sweet potato** (about 1 cup mashed, peeled and cubed)
- **1/2 cup almond butter** (or peanut butter)
- **1/2 cup cocoa powder** (unsweetened)
- **1/4 cup pure maple syrup** or **honey**
- **1/4 cup coconut sugar** or **brown sugar**
- **1/2 teaspoon vanilla extract**
- **1/4 teaspoon salt**
- **1/2 teaspoon baking powder**
- **1/2 cup chocolate chips** (optional, for added richness)
- **Optional add-ins:** nuts, seeds, or dried fruit

Instructions:

1. **Prepare the Sweet Potato:**
    - Preheat your oven to 375°F (190°C).
    - Pierce the sweet potato with a fork and bake on a baking sheet for 45-60 minutes, or until tender. Alternatively, you can microwave it for 5-7 minutes until soft.
    - Let it cool slightly, then peel and mash until smooth.
2. **Prepare the Brownie Batter:**
    - Preheat your oven to 350°F (175°C) and line an 8x8-inch (20x20 cm) baking pan with parchment paper.
    - In a large bowl, mix together the mashed sweet potato, almond butter, cocoa powder, maple syrup, coconut sugar, vanilla extract, salt, and baking powder until smooth and well combined.
    - Fold in the chocolate chips if using.
3. **Bake the Brownies:**
    - Pour the batter into the prepared baking pan and spread evenly with a spatula.
    - Bake in the preheated oven for 25-30 minutes, or until a toothpick inserted into the center comes out mostly clean (a few moist crumbs are okay).
4. **Cool and Slice:**
    - Allow the brownies to cool in the pan for about 10 minutes, then lift them out using the parchment paper and transfer to a wire rack to cool completely.
    - Once completely cooled, cut into squares.
5. **Serve:**
    - Enjoy your sweet potato brownies as a healthy treat or dessert.

Tips:

- **Sweet Potato:** Make sure the sweet potato is well-mashed to avoid lumps in the brownies.

- **Texture:** For a fudgier brownie, you can use almond flour instead of all-purpose flour. For a richer texture, add extra chocolate chips or nuts.
- **Storage:** Store the brownies in an airtight container at room temperature for up to 4 days, or refrigerate for longer freshness. They can also be frozen for up to 3 months.

These sweet potato brownies are a nutritious and tasty way to enjoy a classic dessert with a healthier twist. Enjoy your baking!

Maple Pecan Granola

Ingredients:

- **2 cups old-fashioned rolled oats**
- **1 cup pecans** (chopped or whole, depending on preference)
- **1/2 cup almonds** (chopped, optional)
- **1/4 cup sunflower seeds** (optional)
- **1/4 cup pumpkin seeds** (optional)
- **1/2 cup pure maple syrup**
- **1/4 cup coconut oil** (or any neutral oil like vegetable oil)
- **1/4 cup brown sugar** (lightly packed)
- **1/2 teaspoon vanilla extract**
- **1/2 teaspoon ground cinnamon**
- **1/4 teaspoon salt**
- **1/2 cup dried fruit** (such as cranberries, raisins, or apricots, optional)

Instructions:

1. **Preheat Oven:**
   - Preheat your oven to 325°F (165°C).
   - Line a large baking sheet with parchment paper or a silicone baking mat.
2. **Prepare Dry Ingredients:**
   - In a large bowl, combine the rolled oats, pecans, almonds, sunflower seeds, and pumpkin seeds.
3. **Prepare Wet Ingredients:**
   - In a small saucepan over medium heat, combine the maple syrup, coconut oil, brown sugar, vanilla extract, cinnamon, and salt.
   - Stir until the sugar has dissolved and the mixture is well combined. Remove from heat.
4. **Combine and Mix:**
   - Pour the maple syrup mixture over the dry ingredients.
   - Stir well to coat all the oats and nuts evenly.
5. **Bake:**
   - Spread the granola mixture evenly onto the prepared baking sheet.
   - Bake in the preheated oven for 20-25 minutes, stirring halfway through to ensure even baking.
   - The granola should be golden brown and fragrant. Be careful not to over-bake, as it can burn quickly.
6. **Add Dried Fruit:**
   - Remove the granola from the oven and let it cool completely on the baking sheet.
   - Once cooled, stir in the dried fruit if using.
7. **Store:**
   - Store the granola in an airtight container at room temperature for up to 2 weeks. It can also be frozen for up to 3 months.

8. **Serve:**
    - Enjoy your maple pecan granola with yogurt, milk, or just as a snack on its own.

Tips:

- **Customization:** Feel free to customize the granola with your favorite nuts, seeds, or dried fruits. You can also add a pinch of nutmeg or cardamom for extra flavor.
- **Clumping:** For clumpier granola, press the mixture down with a spatula before baking and avoid stirring too much during baking.
- **Sweetness:** Adjust the sweetness to your preference by varying the amount of maple syrup or brown sugar.

This maple pecan granola is not only delicious but also a nutritious addition to your breakfast routine or as a crunchy snack throughout the day. Enjoy!

Cinnamon Roasted Almonds

Ingredients:

- **2 cups raw almonds** (whole or sliced)
- **1 tablespoon coconut oil** (or olive oil)
- **1/4 cup granulated sugar** (or coconut sugar for a healthier option)
- **1 tablespoon ground cinnamon**
- **1/4 teaspoon salt**

Instructions:

1. **Preheat Oven:**
   - Preheat your oven to 350°F (175°C).
   - Line a baking sheet with parchment paper or a silicone baking mat for easy cleanup.
2. **Prepare Almonds:**
   - In a large bowl, combine the raw almonds with the melted coconut oil. Stir to coat the almonds evenly.
3. **Mix Cinnamon Sugar:**
   - In a small bowl, mix together the granulated sugar, ground cinnamon, and salt.
4. **Coat Almonds:**
   - Sprinkle the cinnamon sugar mixture over the almonds and stir until they are evenly coated.
5. **Roast Almonds:**
   - Spread the coated almonds in a single layer on the prepared baking sheet.
   - Roast in the preheated oven for 10-15 minutes, stirring halfway through to ensure even roasting. Watch closely to avoid burning.
6. **Cool:**
   - Remove the almonds from the oven and let them cool completely on the baking sheet. They will become crispier as they cool.
7. **Store:**
   - Store the cooled almonds in an airtight container at room temperature for up to 2 weeks. They can also be frozen for longer storage.
8. **Serve:**
   - Enjoy your cinnamon roasted almonds as a snack or use them as a flavorful addition to salads, oatmeal, or yogurt.

Tips:

- **Even Roasting:** Make sure the almonds are in a single layer on the baking sheet to ensure even roasting.
- **Variations:** You can experiment with other spices such as nutmeg or cloves for different flavor profiles.

- **Sweetness Level:** Adjust the amount of sugar to suit your taste. You can also use honey or maple syrup instead of granulated sugar for a different flavor.

These cinnamon roasted almonds are a delightful, aromatic snack that's both satisfying and easy to prepare. Enjoy making and snacking on them!

Chia Seed Strawberry Jam

Ingredients:

- **2 cups fresh strawberries** (hulled and sliced, or you can use frozen strawberries, thawed)
- **2 tablespoons honey** or **maple syrup** (adjust to taste; you can also use granulated sugar if preferred)
- **1 tablespoon lemon juice** (freshly squeezed)
- **2 tablespoons chia seeds**
- **Optional:** 1/2 teaspoon vanilla extract (for extra flavor)

Instructions:

1. **Prepare the Strawberries:**
    - If using fresh strawberries, rinse them well, hull, and slice them into small pieces. If using frozen strawberries, thaw and drain them.
2. **Cook the Strawberries:**
    - In a medium saucepan, add the strawberries and honey (or maple syrup). Cook over medium heat, stirring occasionally, until the strawberries start to break down and release their juices, about 5-7 minutes.
3. **Mash the Strawberries:**
    - Use a potato masher or the back of a spoon to mash the strawberries to your desired consistency. For a smoother jam, you can use an immersion blender to blend the mixture.
4. **Add Lemon Juice and Chia Seeds:**
    - Stir in the lemon juice and chia seeds. Continue to cook for another 2-3 minutes, stirring frequently. The chia seeds will absorb the liquid and help thicken the jam.
5. **Cool and Thicken:**
    - Remove the saucepan from heat. Let the jam cool for about 10 minutes; it will continue to thicken as it cools.
6. **Add Optional Vanilla:**
    - If desired, stir in vanilla extract for additional flavor.
7. **Store:**
    - Transfer the cooled jam to a clean jar or airtight container. Store in the refrigerator for up to 2 weeks.
8. **Serve:**
    - Enjoy your chia seed strawberry jam on toast, yogurt, oatmeal, or as a filling for baked goods.

Tips:

- **Sweetness:** Adjust the amount of honey or maple syrup according to your taste and the sweetness of your strawberries.

- **Consistency:** If you prefer a thicker jam, add an extra tablespoon of chia seeds or cook the mixture a bit longer to reduce more liquid.
- **Variations:** You can add other fruits such as raspberries or blueberries for different flavors. Adjust the sweetness and lemon juice as needed for different fruits.

This chia seed strawberry jam is not only easy to make but also packed with nutrients from chia seeds and fresh fruit. Enjoy making and savoring this healthy spread!

Raw Chocolate Protein Balls

Ingredients:

- **1 cup pitted dates** (soaked in warm water for 10 minutes if they are too dry)
- **1/2 cup raw almonds** (or almond flour for a smoother texture)
- **1/4 cup unsweetened cocoa powder**
- **1/4 cup protein powder** (chocolate or vanilla flavor, optional)
- **2 tablespoons chia seeds** (optional, for added nutrition)
- **2 tablespoons coconut oil** (melted)
- **1 teaspoon vanilla extract**
- **Pinch of sea salt**

Instructions:

1. **Prepare Ingredients:**
   - If the dates are dry, soak them in warm water for about 10 minutes, then drain and pat dry.
   - If using whole almonds, process them in a food processor until finely ground.
2. **Process the Ingredients:**
   - In a food processor, combine the pitted dates, ground almonds (or almond flour), cocoa powder, protein powder (if using), chia seeds (if using), melted coconut oil, vanilla extract, and a pinch of sea salt.
   - Process until the mixture is well combined and forms a sticky dough. You may need to stop and scrape down the sides of the processor a few times.
3. **Form the Balls:**
   - Once the mixture is well combined, use your hands or a small cookie scoop to form small balls, about 1 inch in diameter.
4. **Chill:**
   - Place the protein balls on a plate or tray lined with parchment paper.
   - Chill in the refrigerator for at least 30 minutes to firm up.
5. **Serve:**
   - Enjoy the protein balls as a quick snack or energy boost. They can be stored in an airtight container in the refrigerator for up to 2 weeks.
6. **Optional Coatings:**
   - If desired, roll the protein balls in shredded coconut, crushed nuts, or additional cocoa powder for added texture and flavor.

Tips:

- **Dates:** Ensure the dates are soft and sticky for easy blending. If they're too dry, soak them as mentioned.
- **Texture:** For a smoother texture, use almond flour instead of whole almonds. You can also adjust the consistency by adding a little more coconut oil if needed.

- **Protein Powder:** Adjust the amount of protein powder based on your dietary needs and flavor preference. You can omit it if you prefer a simpler recipe.
- **Flavor Variations:** Feel free to add other flavorings like cinnamon, a pinch of espresso powder, or a few drops of mint extract for a different twist.

These raw chocolate protein balls are a versatile, healthy, and satisfying snack that's easy to make and perfect for on-the-go. Enjoy your homemade treat!

Homemade Fruit Sorbet

Ingredients:

- **4 cups fresh or frozen fruit** (such as berries, mango, peach, or pineapple)
- **1/2 cup granulated sugar** (or to taste, you can also use honey, maple syrup, or a sugar substitute)
- **1/2 cup water** (or fruit juice for added flavor)
- **2 tablespoons lemon juice** (freshly squeezed, or lime juice for a different twist)
- **Optional:** 1-2 tablespoons of liqueur (such as fruit liqueur or vodka) to help keep the sorbet soft and scoopable

Instructions:

1. **Prepare the Fruit:**
    - If using fresh fruit, wash and peel it as necessary. For frozen fruit, ensure it is well frozen and can be easily blended.
2. **Blend Ingredients:**
    - In a blender or food processor, combine the fruit, granulated sugar, and water (or fruit juice). Blend until smooth. If you prefer a sweeter sorbet, you can adjust the amount of sugar according to your taste.
3. **Add Lemon Juice:**
    - Add the lemon juice to the fruit mixture and blend again until fully incorporated.
4. **Optional Liqueur:**
    - If using, add the liqueur and blend. This step is optional but helps prevent the sorbet from freezing too hard.
5. **Freeze:**
    - Pour the mixture into a shallow dish or a freezer-safe container. Place it in the freezer.
6. **Stir and Serve:**
    - After about 1 hour, stir the sorbet with a fork to break up any ice crystals. Continue to freeze, stirring every 30 minutes for the next 2-3 hours until the sorbet is firm but still scoopable.
7. **Serve:**
    - Let the sorbet sit at room temperature for a few minutes before serving to soften slightly if needed. Scoop into bowls or cones and enjoy!

Tips:

- **Fruit Choice:** Use ripe fruit for the best flavor. If the fruit is too tart, you can adjust the sweetness with more sugar or a sweetener of your choice.
- **Texture:** If you prefer a smoother sorbet, you can strain the fruit mixture through a fine mesh sieve before freezing to remove any seeds or pulp.
- **Storage:** Store leftover sorbet in an airtight container in the freezer. It's best enjoyed within a week or two for optimal texture and flavor.

This homemade fruit sorbet is a versatile recipe that allows you to experiment with different fruits and flavor combinations, creating a refreshing and naturally sweet treat that's perfect for any occasion. Enjoy!

Coconut-Almond Truffles

Ingredients:

- **1 cup shredded coconut** (unsweetened or sweetened, depending on preference)
- **1/2 cup almond meal** (or finely chopped almonds)
- **1/4 cup coconut oil** (melted)
- **1/4 cup almond butter** (or any nut butter)
- **1/4 cup honey** or **maple syrup**
- **1/2 teaspoon vanilla extract**
- **Pinch of sea salt**
- **Optional:** Extra shredded coconut for rolling

Instructions:

1. **Prepare the Mixture:**
   - In a large bowl, combine the shredded coconut, almond meal, melted coconut oil, almond butter, honey (or maple syrup), vanilla extract, and a pinch of sea salt. Mix well until the ingredients are fully combined and form a sticky dough.
2. **Form the Truffles:**
   - Use your hands or a small cookie scoop to form the mixture into small balls, about 1 inch in diameter.
3. **Coat the Truffles:**
   - If desired, roll each truffle in additional shredded coconut to coat. This adds texture and enhances the coconut flavor.
4. **Chill:**
   - Place the truffles on a plate or tray lined with parchment paper. Chill in the refrigerator for at least 30 minutes to firm up.
5. **Serve:**
   - Enjoy the truffles chilled. They can be stored in an airtight container in the refrigerator for up to 2 weeks or frozen for longer storage.

Tips:

- **Texture:** If the mixture is too dry, add a little more melted coconut oil or almond butter. If it's too wet, add a bit more almond meal or shredded coconut.
- **Flavor Variations:** You can customize the truffles by adding ingredients like cocoa powder, a pinch of sea salt, or a few drops of essential oil (like almond or coconut) for extra flavor.
- **Nut Options:** If you prefer, you can use other nut butters or finely chopped nuts in place of almond butter and almonds.

These coconut-almond truffles are a delicious, no-bake treat that's both rich and satisfying. Enjoy making and sharing these delightful bites!

Apple Nachos with Almond Butter

Ingredients:

- **2 large apples** (such as Honeycrisp, Fuji, or Granny Smith)
- **1/4 cup almond butter** (smooth or crunchy, as preferred)
- **2 tablespoons honey** (or maple syrup, optional for extra sweetness)
- **1/4 cup granola** (for crunch, optional)
- **1/4 cup chopped nuts** (such as almonds, walnuts, or pecans, optional)
- **1/4 cup dried fruit** (such as cranberries, raisins, or shredded coconut, optional)
- **1/4 teaspoon ground cinnamon** (optional, for extra flavor)
- **Mini chocolate chips** or **cacao nibs** (optional, for a touch of indulgence)

Instructions:

1. **Prepare the Apples:**
   - Wash and core the apples. Slice them into thin rounds or thin wedges, removing any seeds. For a more uniform appearance, you can use a mandoline slicer if available.
2. **Arrange the Apple Slices:**
   - Arrange the apple slices in a single layer on a large plate or platter.
3. **Add Almond Butter:**
   - Warm the almond butter slightly if it's too thick (microwave for 10-15 seconds if needed). Drizzle or spoon the almond butter evenly over the apple slices.
4. **Add Toppings:**
   - Drizzle honey or maple syrup over the apple slices for added sweetness if desired.
   - Sprinkle granola, chopped nuts, dried fruit, and ground cinnamon over the almond butter-covered apple slices.
   - Add mini chocolate chips or cacao nibs for a sweet touch if you like.
5. **Serve:**
   - Serve immediately for the freshest taste. Enjoy your apple nachos as a healthy snack or a light dessert.

Tips:

- **Apple Choice:** Use crisp apples that don't brown too quickly to ensure the nachos stay fresh and appealing.
- **Almond Butter:** You can substitute almond butter with other nut butters like peanut butter or cashew butter if preferred.
- **Customization:** Feel free to experiment with different toppings, such as seeds, fresh berries, or a sprinkle of sea salt for added flavor.

These apple nachos with almond butter offer a crunchy, satisfying, and nutritious snack that's easy to prepare and perfect for sharing with friends and family. Enjoy!

Berry-Packed Crumble

Ingredients:

For the Berry Filling:

- **4 cups mixed berries** (fresh or frozen, such as strawberries, blueberries, raspberries, blackberries)
- **1/4 cup granulated sugar** (adjust to taste, depending on the sweetness of the berries)
- **1 tablespoon cornstarch** (or arrowroot powder for thickening)
- **1 tablespoon lemon juice** (freshly squeezed)
- **1 teaspoon vanilla extract** (optional)

For the Crumble Topping:

- **1/2 cup all-purpose flour** (or use almond flour for a gluten-free option)
- **1/2 cup rolled oats**
- **1/3 cup brown sugar** (lightly packed)
- **1/4 teaspoon ground cinnamon**
- **1/4 teaspoon salt**
- **1/4 cup unsalted butter** (cold and cut into small cubes, or use coconut oil for a dairy-free version)

Instructions:

1. **Preheat Oven:**
   - Preheat your oven to 350°F (175°C).
2. **Prepare the Berry Filling:**
   - In a large bowl, combine the mixed berries, granulated sugar, cornstarch, lemon juice, and vanilla extract if using. Gently toss to coat the berries evenly.
   - Transfer the berry mixture to a greased 8x8-inch (20x20 cm) baking dish or similar oven-safe dish.
3. **Prepare the Crumble Topping:**
   - In a medium bowl, mix together the flour, rolled oats, brown sugar, ground cinnamon, and salt.
   - Add the cold butter or coconut oil to the dry ingredients. Using a pastry cutter, fork, or your fingers, work the butter into the mixture until it resembles coarse crumbs.
4. **Assemble the Crumble:**
   - Sprinkle the crumble topping evenly over the berry filling in the baking dish.
5. **Bake:**
   - Bake in the preheated oven for 35-40 minutes, or until the topping is golden brown and the berry filling is bubbling and thickened.
6. **Cool and Serve:**

- Allow the crumble to cool for about 10 minutes before serving. This helps the filling set and makes it easier to scoop.
7. **Serve:**
   - Serve warm or at room temperature. It's delicious on its own or with a scoop of vanilla ice cream or a dollop of whipped cream.

Tips:

- **Berry Mixture:** Feel free to mix and match different types of berries based on what you have available or your personal preference.
- **Sweetness Level:** Adjust the amount of sugar in both the berry filling and crumble topping to suit your taste and the sweetness of your berries.
- **Gluten-Free:** Use gluten-free flour and ensure your oats are certified gluten-free if you need to make this recipe gluten-free.

Berry-packed crumble is a comforting and versatile dessert that celebrates the flavors of fresh berries with a crunchy topping. Enjoy making and sharing this delightful treat!

Coconut-Date Energy Bars

Ingredients:

- **1 1/2 cups pitted dates** (packed, preferably Medjool dates for their softness)
- **1 cup shredded coconut** (unsweetened or sweetened, based on preference)
- **1/2 cup nuts** (such as almonds, cashews, or walnuts, roughly chopped)
- **1/4 cup nut butter** (such as almond butter, cashew butter, or peanut butter)
- **2 tablespoons coconut oil** (melted)
- **1 teaspoon vanilla extract**
- **Pinch of sea salt**
- **Optional:** 2 tablespoons chia seeds or flaxseeds for added nutrition

Instructions:

1. **Prepare the Dates:**
   - If the dates are too dry, soak them in warm water for 10 minutes, then drain and pat dry. This will help them blend more easily.
2. **Blend Ingredients:**
   - In a food processor, combine the pitted dates, shredded coconut, and chopped nuts. Process until the mixture is finely chopped and starts to clump together.
3. **Add Remaining Ingredients:**
   - Add the nut butter, melted coconut oil, vanilla extract, and a pinch of sea salt to the food processor. If using chia seeds or flaxseeds, add them here. Process until the mixture is well combined and forms a sticky dough.
4. **Press into Pan:**
   - Line an 8x8-inch (20x20 cm) baking dish with parchment paper or lightly grease it. Transfer the mixture to the prepared dish and press it down evenly using your hands or the back of a spoon.
5. **Chill:**
   - Refrigerate the mixture for at least 1-2 hours to firm up. This will make it easier to cut into bars.
6. **Cut and Serve:**
   - Once firm, lift the mixture out of the pan using the parchment paper and cut it into bars or squares.
7. **Store:**
   - Store the energy bars in an airtight container in the refrigerator for up to 2 weeks. They can also be frozen for up to 3 months.

Tips:

- **Sweetness Level:** Adjust the sweetness by adding more dates or a bit of honey if desired. The sweetness will also depend on the type of dates and nut butter used.
- **Texture:** For a smoother texture, you can blend the nuts into a finer meal or use nut flour instead.

- **Add-Ins:** Feel free to customize the bars by adding ingredients like chocolate chips, dried fruit, or a sprinkle of cinnamon for extra flavor.

These coconut-date energy bars are a delicious, wholesome snack that's easy to prepare and perfect for keeping your energy levels up throughout the day. Enjoy making and snacking on these tasty bars!

Frozen Fruit Bars

Ingredients:

- **2 cups fresh or frozen fruit** (such as berries, mango, pineapple, or peaches)
- **1/4 cup honey** or **maple syrup** (adjust to taste; you can also use agave syrup or a sugar substitute)
- **1/4 cup freshly squeezed lemon juice** (or lime juice for a different flavor)
- **1/2 cup Greek yogurt** (plain or vanilla; optional, for creaminess)
- **1/4 cup water** (or fruit juice for extra flavor)

Instructions:

1. **Prepare the Fruit:**
    - If using fresh fruit, wash and cut it into chunks. If using frozen fruit, make sure it's thawed slightly for easier blending.
2. **Blend Ingredients:**
    - In a blender or food processor, combine the fruit, honey (or maple syrup), lemon juice, Greek yogurt (if using), and water (or fruit juice). Blend until smooth.
3. **Taste and Adjust:**
    - Taste the mixture and adjust the sweetness or acidity if needed by adding more honey/maple syrup or lemon juice. Blend again to mix.
4. **Pour into Molds:**
    - Pour the fruit mixture into silicone ice pop molds, plastic cups, or paper cups. If using cups, insert sticks once the mixture is partially frozen (about 1-2 hours) so they stay upright.
5. **Freeze:**
    - Place the molds or cups in the freezer and freeze for at least 4 hours or until solid.
6. **Unmold and Serve:**
    - To remove the bars from the molds, run warm water over the outside of the molds for a few seconds to help release them. Serve immediately.
7. **Store:**
    - Store leftover frozen fruit bars in an airtight container in the freezer. They should stay good for up to 2-3 months.

Tips:

- **Fruit Combinations:** Experiment with different fruit combinations to create unique flavors. For example, you can blend berries with a bit of banana, or mix mango with pineapple.
- **Creaminess:** Adding Greek yogurt makes the bars creamier. For a dairy-free option, you can use coconut yogurt or skip the yogurt altogether.
- **Add-Ins:** You can mix in chopped nuts, shredded coconut, or mini chocolate chips for added texture and flavor.

These frozen fruit bars are a healthy, easy-to-make treat that's perfect for cooling down on a hot day or satisfying your sweet tooth in a nutritious way. Enjoy making and indulging in these refreshing bars!

Baked Cinnamon Apples

Ingredients:

- **4 medium apples** (such as Honeycrisp, Fuji, or Gala)
- **1/4 cup brown sugar** (lightly packed; adjust to taste)
- **1 teaspoon ground cinnamon**
- **1/4 teaspoon ground nutmeg** (optional)
- **2 tablespoons unsalted butter** (or coconut oil for a dairy-free option)
- **1/4 cup chopped nuts** (such as walnuts or pecans, optional)
- **1/4 cup raisins or dried cranberries** (optional)
- **1/2 cup water** or **apple juice**

Instructions:

1. **Preheat Oven:**
   - Preheat your oven to 350°F (175°C).
2. **Prepare the Apples:**
   - Wash, peel (optional), and core the apples. You can leave the apples whole or cut them into wedges or slices, depending on your preference.
3. **Make the Cinnamon Mixture:**
   - In a small bowl, mix together the brown sugar, ground cinnamon, and ground nutmeg (if using).
4. **Stuff the Apples:**
   - If leaving the apples whole, place them in a baking dish. Stuff the centers with the cinnamon mixture, chopped nuts, and raisins or dried cranberries (if using).
   - If cutting the apples into wedges or slices, toss them with the cinnamon mixture, nuts, and dried fruit, and then spread them out in an even layer in the baking dish.
5. **Add Butter and Liquid:**
   - Dot the apples with small pieces of butter or drizzle with melted coconut oil.
   - Pour the water or apple juice into the bottom of the baking dish to help create steam and keep the apples moist during baking.
6. **Bake:**
   - Bake in the preheated oven for 30-40 minutes, or until the apples are tender and the topping is golden brown. If baking whole apples, the baking time may be a bit longer.
7. **Serve:**
   - Serve warm, on its own or with a scoop of vanilla ice cream, a dollop of yogurt, or a sprinkle of granola.

Tips:

- **Apple Choice:** Choose apples that hold their shape well during baking, such as Honeycrisp or Fuji. Softer apples like McIntosh may become mushy.

- **Sweetness Level:** Adjust the amount of brown sugar based on the sweetness of your apples and your personal preference. You can also use maple syrup or honey as an alternative sweetener.
- **Flavor Variations:** Add a splash of vanilla extract to the cinnamon mixture or a drizzle of caramel sauce before serving for extra flavor.

Baked cinnamon apples are a classic and easy dessert that brings out the natural flavors of apples with a comforting, spiced touch. Enjoy making and savoring this delicious treat!

Avocado Lime Cheesecake

Ingredients:

For the Crust:

- **1 cup graham cracker crumbs** (or use gluten-free crumbs if needed)
- **1/4 cup coconut oil** (melted, or unsalted butter for a non-dairy option)
- **2 tablespoons honey** or **maple syrup** (for sweetness)

For the Filling:

- **2 ripe avocados** (peeled and pitted)
- **1/2 cup lime juice** (freshly squeezed)
- **1/4 cup honey** or **maple syrup** (adjust to taste)
- **1/4 cup coconut milk** (full-fat for creaminess; you can also use heavy cream)
- **1 teaspoon vanilla extract**
- **1/2 teaspoon lime zest** (optional, for extra flavor)
- **1 teaspoon gelatin powder** (or agar-agar for a vegetarian option, optional for setting; use 1 tablespoon of agar-agar if using)

For Garnish:

- **Fresh lime slices** or **zest**
- **Shredded coconut** (toasted, optional)
- **Fresh mint leaves** (optional)

Instructions:

1. **Prepare the Crust:**
    - In a medium bowl, combine the graham cracker crumbs, melted coconut oil, and honey or maple syrup. Mix until the crumbs are evenly coated and the mixture resembles wet sand.
    - Press the mixture into the bottom of a 9-inch (23 cm) springform pan or pie dish to form an even layer. Use the back of a spoon to press it down firmly.
    - Place the crust in the refrigerator while you prepare the filling.
2. **Prepare the Filling:**
    - In a blender or food processor, combine the ripe avocados, lime juice, honey or maple syrup, coconut milk, vanilla extract, and lime zest (if using). Blend until smooth and creamy.
    - If using gelatin, dissolve it in 2 tablespoons of warm water, then add to the blender and blend again until fully incorporated. If using agar-agar, follow the package instructions to dissolve it in hot water, then mix into the filling.
3. **Assemble the Cheesecake:**
    - Pour the avocado lime filling over the prepared crust, spreading it out evenly with a spatula.

- Refrigerate for at least 4 hours, or until the cheesecake is set. For best results, leave it overnight.
4. **Garnish and Serve:**
    - Before serving, garnish with fresh lime slices or zest, toasted shredded coconut, and fresh mint leaves if desired.
    - Slice and serve chilled.

Tips:

- **Texture:** If you prefer a firmer texture, add more gelatin or agar-agar as needed. For a creamier texture, ensure the avocados are very ripe and blend the filling thoroughly.
- **Sweetness:** Adjust the amount of honey or maple syrup to taste, depending on how sweet or tart you prefer your cheesecake.
- **Variations:** You can experiment with other citrus fruits, like lemon or orange, for a different flavor profile.

This avocado lime cheesecake is a refreshing, healthier alternative to traditional cheesecake, perfect for a light and satisfying dessert. Enjoy making and indulging in this delicious treat!

Almond Flour Pancakes

Ingredients:

- **2 cups almond flour**
- **1/4 cup arrowroot powder** or **tapioca flour** (for fluffiness; optional)
- **1/2 teaspoon baking powder**
- **1/4 teaspoon salt**
- **3 large eggs**
- **1/4 cup milk** (or non-dairy milk like almond milk)
- **2 tablespoons honey** or **maple syrup**
- **1 teaspoon vanilla extract**
- **2 tablespoons coconut oil** or **butter** (for cooking)

Instructions:

1. **Prepare the Dry Ingredients:**
   - In a large bowl, whisk together the almond flour, arrowroot powder (if using), baking powder, and salt.
2. **Mix the Wet Ingredients:**
   - In another bowl, beat the eggs. Then add the milk, honey (or maple syrup), and vanilla extract. Mix well.
3. **Combine Ingredients:**
   - Pour the wet ingredients into the dry ingredients and stir until just combined. The batter will be thick, but it should hold together well.
4. **Heat the Pan:**
   - Heat a non-stick skillet or griddle over medium-low heat. Add a little coconut oil or butter to coat the pan.
5. **Cook the Pancakes:**
   - For each pancake, pour about 1/4 cup of batter onto the skillet. Use the back of a spoon to spread it into a round shape. Cook for 2-3 minutes, or until bubbles form on the surface and the edges look set. Flip the pancake and cook for another 1-2 minutes, or until golden brown and cooked through.
6. **Serve:**
   - Remove the pancakes from the skillet and keep warm. Repeat with the remaining batter, adding more oil or butter to the pan as needed.
7. **Top and Enjoy:**
   - Serve the pancakes warm with your favorite toppings, such as fresh fruit, maple syrup, yogurt, or a sprinkle of nuts.

Tips:

- **Consistency:** If the batter is too thick, you can add a bit more milk to reach your desired consistency.

- **Flavor Variations:** Add mix-ins such as blueberries, chocolate chips, or chopped nuts to the batter before cooking for extra flavor.
- **Storage:** These pancakes can be stored in the refrigerator for a few days or frozen for longer storage. Reheat in a toaster or skillet.

Almond flour pancakes are a versatile and tasty breakfast option that's perfect for those following a gluten-free or low-carb diet. Enjoy making and savoring these delicious, nutty pancakes!

Peach Coconut Muffins

Ingredients:

- **1 1/2 cups all-purpose flour** (or use a gluten-free blend if needed)
- **1/2 cup shredded coconut** (sweetened or unsweetened, depending on preference)
- **1/2 cup granulated sugar** (or coconut sugar for a healthier option)
- **1/2 teaspoon baking powder**
- **1/2 teaspoon baking soda**
- **1/4 teaspoon salt**
- **1/2 cup coconut oil** (melted; or use vegetable oil)
- **1/2 cup milk** (or non-dairy milk such as almond milk)
- **1 large egg**
- **1 teaspoon vanilla extract**
- **1 cup fresh or frozen peaches** (diced; thaw if using frozen and pat dry)
- **Optional:** 1/4 cup chopped nuts (such as pecans or walnuts) for added crunch

Instructions:

1. **Preheat Oven:**
   - Preheat your oven to 350°F (175°C). Line a muffin tin with paper liners or grease the cups lightly.
2. **Prepare Dry Ingredients:**
   - In a large bowl, whisk together the flour, shredded coconut, granulated sugar, baking powder, baking soda, and salt.
3. **Mix Wet Ingredients:**
   - In another bowl, whisk together the melted coconut oil, milk, egg, and vanilla extract until well combined.
4. **Combine Ingredients:**
   - Pour the wet ingredients into the dry ingredients and stir until just combined. Be careful not to overmix.
   - Gently fold in the diced peaches and chopped nuts (if using).
5. **Fill Muffin Cups:**
   - Divide the batter evenly among the muffin cups, filling each about 2/3 full.
6. **Bake:**
   - Bake in the preheated oven for 20-25 minutes, or until the muffins are golden brown and a toothpick inserted into the center comes out clean.
7. **Cool:**
   - Allow the muffins to cool in the tin for about 5 minutes, then transfer them to a wire rack to cool completely.
8. **Serve:**
   - Enjoy the muffins warm or at room temperature. They are perfect for breakfast, a snack, or a light dessert.

Tips:

- **Peach Preparation:** If using fresh peaches, make sure they are ripe and juicy for the best flavor. If using frozen peaches, ensure they are well-drained to avoid excess moisture in the batter.
- **Texture:** For a more tender crumb, consider sifting the flour before measuring.
- **Sweetness:** Adjust the sugar to taste based on the sweetness of your peaches and personal preference.

Peach coconut muffins are a wonderful way to enjoy the flavors of summer with a moist and flavorful treat. Enjoy baking and savoring these delicious muffins!

Walnut Date Balls

Ingredients:

- **1 cup walnuts** (or other nuts like almonds or pecans, if preferred)
- **1 cup pitted dates** (preferably Medjool dates for their softness)
- **2 tablespoons coconut oil** (or almond oil for a different flavor, optional)
- **1/4 teaspoon vanilla extract** (optional)
- **A pinch of salt** (optional, to enhance flavor)
- **1/4 cup shredded coconut** (for rolling, optional)

Instructions:

1. **Prepare the Nuts:**
   - Place the walnuts in a food processor and pulse until finely chopped. You want them to be small but not turned into a meal. Set aside.
2. **Process the Dates:**
   - In the same food processor, add the pitted dates. Process until they form a sticky, paste-like consistency. If the dates are too dry, you can add a little bit of water or coconut oil to help them blend.
3. **Combine Ingredients:**
   - Add the chopped walnuts to the processed dates. If using, also add the coconut oil, vanilla extract, and a pinch of salt. Pulse until the mixture is well combined and the nuts are mixed evenly with the date paste. The mixture should hold together when pressed.
4. **Form the Balls:**
   - Scoop out small amounts of the mixture (about 1 tablespoon each) and roll them into balls using your hands. If the mixture is too sticky, lightly wet your hands to make rolling easier.
5. **Optional Rolling:**
   - Roll the balls in shredded coconut if you like. This adds a nice texture and extra flavor. You can also roll them in cocoa powder, crushed nuts, or a mix of spices like cinnamon if desired.
6. **Chill and Store:**
   - Place the rolled date balls on a parchment-lined tray or plate. Refrigerate for at least 30 minutes to firm up. Store in an airtight container in the refrigerator for up to 2 weeks or freeze for up to 3 months.

Tips:

- **Texture:** If the mixture is too dry and crumbly, add a bit more coconut oil or a small amount of water to help it come together.
- **Variations:** You can add other ingredients like chia seeds, flaxseeds, or a pinch of cinnamon to customize the flavor and boost the nutritional content.

- **Sweetness Level:** Adjust the sweetness by adding more dates or a small amount of honey or maple syrup if desired.

These walnut date balls are a nutritious, energy-boosting snack that's perfect for a quick pick-me-up or a healthy treat to satisfy your sweet tooth. Enjoy making and snacking on these delicious bites!

Carrot Cake Bites

Ingredients:

- **1 cup finely grated carrots** (about 2 medium carrots, peeled and grated)
- **1 cup rolled oats** (or use quick oats for a finer texture)
- **1/2 cup finely chopped nuts** (such as walnuts or pecans)
- **1/2 cup pitted dates** (preferably Medjool dates for their softness)
- **1/4 cup shredded coconut** (unsweetened or sweetened, depending on preference)
- **1/4 cup raisins** or **dried cranberries** (optional, for extra sweetness)
- **1/2 teaspoon ground cinnamon**
- **1/4 teaspoon ground nutmeg**
- **1/4 teaspoon ground ginger** (optional, for extra spice)
- **1 tablespoon maple syrup** or **honey** (optional, for added sweetness)
- **1-2 tablespoons coconut oil** (optional, for binding and richness)

Instructions:

1. **Prepare the Ingredients:**
   - If the dates are dry, soak them in warm water for 10 minutes, then drain and pat dry. This will help them blend more easily.
2. **Blend the Mixture:**
   - In a food processor, combine the grated carrots, rolled oats, chopped nuts, dates, shredded coconut, raisins (if using), cinnamon, nutmeg, and ginger (if using). Process until the mixture is well combined and forms a sticky dough-like consistency. If the mixture is too dry, add a tablespoon of coconut oil or a bit of maple syrup/honey to help it come together.
3. **Form the Bites:**
   - Scoop out small amounts of the mixture (about 1 tablespoon each) and roll them into balls using your hands. If the mixture is too sticky, lightly wet your hands or refrigerate the mixture for a few minutes to make rolling easier.
4. **Chill:**
   - Place the rolled bites on a parchment-lined tray or plate. Refrigerate for at least 30 minutes to firm up.
5. **Store:**
   - Store the carrot cake bites in an airtight container in the refrigerator for up to 2 weeks. They can also be frozen for up to 3 months.

Tips:

- **Texture:** If the mixture is too crumbly, add a bit more coconut oil or a small amount of water to help it stick together.
- **Customization:** Feel free to add other ingredients such as chia seeds, flaxseeds, or a sprinkle of walnuts on the outside for extra texture.

- **Sweetness:** Adjust the sweetness to your taste by adding more dates or a bit of maple syrup or honey if desired.

These carrot cake bites are a tasty and healthy alternative to traditional carrot cake, making them a great snack or a light dessert. Enjoy making and savoring these flavorful treats!

Berry Coconut Popsicles

Ingredients:

- **1 cup mixed berries** (such as strawberries, blueberries, raspberries, or blackberries; fresh or frozen)
- **1 cup coconut milk** (full-fat for creaminess; can use canned or carton coconut milk)
- **1/4 cup honey** or **maple syrup** (adjust to taste; you can use other sweeteners if preferred)
- **1 teaspoon vanilla extract** (optional, for extra flavor)
- **1 tablespoon lemon juice** (optional, for a hint of tartness)
- **A handful of whole or chopped berries** (for added texture, optional)

Instructions:

1. **Prepare the Berries:**
    - If using fresh berries, wash them thoroughly. If using frozen berries, allow them to thaw slightly for easier blending.
2. **Blend Ingredients:**
    - In a blender, combine the mixed berries, coconut milk, honey (or maple syrup), vanilla extract (if using), and lemon juice (if using). Blend until smooth.
3. **Add Whole Berries (Optional):**
    - If you'd like to include whole or chopped berries in the popsicles for added texture, gently stir them into the blended mixture.
4. **Pour into Molds:**
    - Pour the berry-coconut mixture into popsicle molds. If using popsicle sticks, insert them into the molds.
5. **Freeze:**
    - Place the molds in the freezer and freeze for at least 4-6 hours, or until the popsicles are completely solid.
6. **Unmold and Serve:**
    - To release the popsicles from the molds, run warm water over the outside of the molds for a few seconds to loosen them. Serve immediately.
7. **Store:**
    - Store any leftover popsicles in the freezer. They should stay good for up to 3 months.

Tips:

- **Berry Variations:** Feel free to experiment with different berry combinations or add other fruits like mango or pineapple for a tropical twist.
- **Sweetness:** Adjust the sweetness to your preference by adding more or less honey or maple syrup. You can also taste the mixture before freezing to ensure it's sweet enough.
- **Texture:** For a creamier popsicle, use full-fat coconut milk. For a lighter version, you can use light coconut milk or a combination of coconut milk and almond milk.

Berry coconut popsicles are a delicious and healthy frozen treat that's easy to make and perfect for cooling down on a hot day. Enjoy making and indulging in these refreshing popsicles!

Cashew Butter Brownies

Ingredients:

- **1/2 cup cashew butter** (smooth, preferably unsweetened)
- **1/4 cup coconut oil** (or unsalted butter, melted)
- **1/2 cup coconut sugar** or **brown sugar** (or granulated sugar)
- **1/4 cup cocoa powder** (unsweetened)
- **2 large eggs**
- **1/2 teaspoon vanilla extract**
- **1/4 teaspoon salt**
- **1/2 teaspoon baking powder**
- **1/4 cup mini chocolate chips** or **chopped nuts** (optional, for extra texture)

Instructions:

1. **Preheat Oven:**
   - Preheat your oven to 350°F (175°C). Grease or line an 8x8-inch baking pan with parchment paper.
2. **Prepare the Wet Ingredients:**
   - In a medium bowl, mix together the cashew butter, melted coconut oil, and coconut sugar until well combined.
3. **Add the Eggs:**
   - Beat in the eggs, one at a time, until fully incorporated. Stir in the vanilla extract.
4. **Mix Dry Ingredients:**
   - In a separate bowl, whisk together the cocoa powder, salt, and baking powder.
5. **Combine Ingredients:**
   - Gradually add the dry ingredients to the wet mixture, stirring until just combined. Be careful not to overmix.
6. **Add Optional Ingredients:**
   - Fold in mini chocolate chips or chopped nuts if using.
7. **Bake:**
   - Pour the batter into the prepared baking pan and spread it evenly.
   - Bake in the preheated oven for 20-25 minutes, or until a toothpick inserted into the center comes out with a few moist crumbs. The brownies should be set but still fudgy in the center.
8. **Cool and Cut:**
   - Allow the brownies to cool in the pan for about 10 minutes before transferring to a wire rack to cool completely. Once cooled, cut into squares.
9. **Serve:**
   - Enjoy the brownies as is, or serve with a scoop of ice cream or a dollop of whipped cream for an extra treat.

Tips:

- **Consistency:** If the batter seems too thick, you can add a splash of milk or a bit more coconut oil to reach the desired consistency.
- **Sweetness:** Adjust the sweetness by adding more or less sugar, based on your preference and the sweetness of your cashew butter.
- **Storage:** Store brownies in an airtight container at room temperature for up to 4-5 days, or refrigerate for up to a week. They can also be frozen for up to 3 months.

These cashew butter brownies are a delicious, nutty twist on traditional brownies, offering a rich and satisfying treat that's perfect for any occasion. Enjoy making and indulging in these tasty brownies!

Coconut Lime Energy Balls

Ingredients:

- **1 cup shredded coconut** (unsweetened, plus extra for rolling)
- **1 cup pitted dates** (preferably Medjool dates for their softness)
- **1/2 cup raw cashews** (or other nuts like almonds or walnuts)
- **1/4 cup lime juice** (freshly squeezed)
- **1 tablespoon lime zest** (from about 1 lime)
- **1 tablespoon coconut oil** (optional, for added richness)
- **1/4 teaspoon vanilla extract** (optional, for extra flavor)
- **A pinch of salt** (optional, to enhance flavor)

Instructions:

1. **Prepare the Ingredients:**
   - If the dates are dry, soak them in warm water for about 10 minutes, then drain and pat dry. This will help them blend more easily.
2. **Blend the Ingredients:**
   - In a food processor, combine the shredded coconut, pitted dates, and cashews. Process until the mixture is finely chopped and begins to come together. The mixture should be slightly sticky.
3. **Add Lime Flavor:**
   - Add the lime juice, lime zest, coconut oil (if using), vanilla extract (if using), and a pinch of salt (if using) to the food processor. Blend again until the mixture is well combined and forms a sticky dough-like consistency. If the mixture is too dry, add a little more lime juice or a bit of water.
4. **Form the Balls:**
   - Scoop out small amounts of the mixture (about 1 tablespoon each) and roll them into balls using your hands. If the mixture is too sticky, lightly wet your hands or refrigerate the mixture for a few minutes to make rolling easier.
5. **Roll in Coconut (Optional):**
   - Roll the balls in additional shredded coconut for a nice coating and extra texture.
6. **Chill:**
   - Place the rolled energy balls on a parchment-lined tray or plate. Refrigerate for at least 30 minutes to firm up.
7. **Store:**
   - Store the energy balls in an airtight container in the refrigerator for up to 2 weeks or freeze for up to 3 months.

Tips:

- **Consistency:** If the mixture is too dry, you can add a bit more lime juice or a small amount of water to help it come together.

- **Sweetness:** Adjust the sweetness to your preference by adding more dates or a bit of honey or maple syrup if desired.
- **Flavor Variations:** Experiment with other flavors by adding a bit of grated ginger, chia seeds, or different nuts.

Coconut lime energy balls are a vibrant and energizing snack that's easy to make and perfect for on-the-go. Enjoy these delicious, healthy bites!

Baked Banana Chips

Ingredients:

- **3-4 ripe but firm bananas** (not overly ripe; slightly underripe is best for crispness)
- **1 tablespoon lemon juice** (to prevent browning and add a touch of tang)
- **1 tablespoon coconut oil** (melted, or use another oil like olive oil if preferred)
- **1/2 teaspoon ground cinnamon** (optional, for extra flavor)
- **1-2 tablespoons honey** or **maple syrup** (optional, for added sweetness)

Instructions:

1. **Preheat Oven:**
   - Preheat your oven to 225°F (110°C). Line a baking sheet with parchment paper or a silicone baking mat.
2. **Prepare the Bananas:**
   - Peel the bananas and slice them thinly (about 1/8 inch thick). Consistent slicing ensures even baking.
3. **Prevent Browning:**
   - In a bowl, toss the banana slices with lemon juice to prevent browning and add a bit of tanginess.
4. **Coat the Bananas:**
   - If using, toss the banana slices with melted coconut oil. This helps them crisp up and adds flavor. You can also add a touch of honey or maple syrup for extra sweetness at this stage.
5. **Arrange on Baking Sheet:**
   - Arrange the banana slices in a single layer on the prepared baking sheet. Make sure they are not overlapping to ensure even baking.
6. **Bake:**
   - Bake in the preheated oven for about 1.5 to 2 hours, flipping the slices halfway through the baking time. The exact time may vary depending on the thickness of the slices and your oven.
7. **Cool:**
   - The banana chips are done when they are crisp and dry. Allow them to cool on the baking sheet. They will continue to harden as they cool.
8. **Store:**
   - Store the cooled banana chips in an airtight container. They should stay fresh for up to 2 weeks. For longer storage, you can keep them in the refrigerator or freezer.

Tips:

- **Uniform Slices:** Use a mandoline slicer if you have one, to ensure uniform thickness and even baking.

- **Texture:** If the banana chips are not as crispy as you'd like after baking, you can place them back in the oven for an additional 10-15 minutes, but keep a close eye to avoid burning.
- **Flavor Variations:** Experiment with different spices like cinnamon, nutmeg, or a sprinkle of sea salt to add variety to your banana chips.

Baked banana chips are a great healthy snack that's easy to make and perfect for satisfying crunchy cravings. Enjoy these homemade treats!

Zucchini Brownies

Ingredients:

- **1 cup finely grated zucchini** (about 1 medium zucchini; make sure to drain excess moisture)
- **1/2 cup coconut oil** (or unsalted butter, melted)
- **1 cup granulated sugar** (or coconut sugar for a healthier option)
- **2 large eggs**
- **1 teaspoon vanilla extract**
- **1/2 cup cocoa powder** (unsweetened)
- **1 cup all-purpose flour** (or a gluten-free blend if needed)
- **1/2 teaspoon baking powder**
- **1/4 teaspoon salt**
- **1/2 cup mini chocolate chips** or **chopped nuts** (optional, for extra texture)

Instructions:

1. **Preheat Oven:**
    - Preheat your oven to 350°F (175°C). Grease or line an 8x8-inch baking pan with parchment paper.
2. **Prepare the Zucchini:**
    - Grate the zucchini and squeeze out excess moisture using a clean kitchen towel or cheesecloth. You want the zucchini to be as dry as possible to avoid excess moisture in the batter.
3. **Mix Wet Ingredients:**
    - In a large bowl, combine the melted coconut oil (or butter) and granulated sugar. Stir until well combined.
    - Beat in the eggs one at a time, then add the vanilla extract.
4. **Combine Dry Ingredients:**
    - In a separate bowl, whisk together the cocoa powder, flour, baking powder, and salt.
5. **Mix Together:**
    - Gradually add the dry ingredients to the wet ingredients, stirring until just combined.
    - Fold in the grated zucchini and mini chocolate chips or nuts if using.
6. **Bake:**
    - Pour the batter into the prepared baking pan and spread it evenly.
    - Bake in the preheated oven for 25-30 minutes, or until a toothpick inserted into the center comes out with a few moist crumbs. The brownies should be set but still fudgy in the center.
7. **Cool and Cut:**
    - Allow the brownies to cool in the pan for about 10 minutes before transferring to a wire rack to cool completely. Once cooled, cut into squares.
8. **Serve:**

- Enjoy the brownies as a delicious, healthier dessert or snack. They are great on their own or served with a scoop of ice cream or a dollop of whipped cream.

Tips:

- **Zucchini Prep:** Make sure to drain the zucchini well to avoid soggy brownies. You can also pat it dry with paper towels after grating.
- **Sweetness:** Adjust the sweetness to your taste by adding more or less sugar, depending on your preference and the sweetness of your cocoa powder.
- **Texture:** If you prefer a smoother brownie, you can blend the zucchini into a finer consistency before adding it to the batter.

Zucchini brownies are a great way to enjoy a classic dessert with an added nutritional boost. They're moist, fudgy, and packed with chocolate flavor. Enjoy baking and indulging in these tasty treats!

Almond Joy Energy Bites

Ingredients:

- **1 cup pitted dates** (preferably Medjool dates for their softness)
- **1 cup unsweetened shredded coconut**
- **1/2 cup raw almonds** (plus extra for topping, if desired)
- **1/4 cup almond butter** (or cashew butter if preferred)
- **1/4 cup cocoa powder** (unsweetened)
- **1 tablespoon coconut oil** (melted, optional, for added richness)
- **1 tablespoon honey** or **maple syrup** (optional, for added sweetness)
- **1/4 teaspoon vanilla extract** (optional, for extra flavor)
- **A pinch of salt** (optional, to enhance flavor)

Instructions:

1. **Prepare the Dates:**
   - If the dates are dry, soak them in warm water for about 10 minutes, then drain and pat dry. This will help them blend more easily.
2. **Blend Ingredients:**
   - In a food processor, combine the pitted dates, shredded coconut, raw almonds, almond butter, cocoa powder, and coconut oil (if using). Blend until the mixture is well combined and forms a sticky dough-like consistency.
3. **Adjust Sweetness and Consistency:**
   - Taste the mixture and adjust the sweetness by adding honey or maple syrup if desired. If the mixture is too dry, add a little more almond butter or a small amount of water.
4. **Form the Bites:**
   - Scoop out small amounts of the mixture (about 1 tablespoon each) and roll them into balls using your hands. If the mixture is too sticky, lightly wet your hands or refrigerate the mixture for a few minutes to make rolling easier.
5. **Add Almonds (Optional):**
   - For a more authentic Almond Joy experience, press a whole almond into the center of each ball, or roll the bites in additional shredded coconut.
6. **Chill:**
   - Place the rolled energy bites on a parchment-lined tray or plate. Refrigerate for at least 30 minutes to firm up.
7. **Store:**
   - Store the energy bites in an airtight container in the refrigerator for up to 2 weeks. They can also be frozen for up to 3 months.

Tips:

- **Texture:** If the mixture is too crumbly, add a bit more almond butter or a small amount of water to help it stick together.

- **Flavor Variations:** You can experiment with adding other ingredients like a sprinkle of sea salt, or a bit of espresso powder for a mocha flavor.
- **Customization:** Use different nuts or nut butters to suit your taste preferences.

Almond Joy energy bites are a delicious, nutritious treat that combines the flavors of chocolate, coconut, and almonds in a convenient, bite-sized form. Enjoy making and snacking on these tasty bites!

Raspberry Coconut Bars

Ingredients:

- **1 1/2 cups shredded coconut** (unsweetened)
- **1 cup almond flour** (or all-purpose flour if preferred)
- **1/4 cup coconut oil** (melted)
- **1/4 cup maple syrup** or **honey** (or to taste)
- **1/2 teaspoon vanilla extract**
- **1/2 cup fresh or frozen raspberries** (thawed if frozen)
- **1 tablespoon chia seeds** (optional, for added texture and nutrition)

Instructions:

1. **Preheat Oven:**
   - Preheat your oven to 350°F (175°C). Grease or line an 8x8-inch baking pan with parchment paper.
2. **Prepare the Crust:**
   - In a mixing bowl, combine the shredded coconut, almond flour, melted coconut oil, maple syrup (or honey), and vanilla extract. Mix until the ingredients are well combined and form a crumbly dough.
3. **Press into Pan:**
   - Press the mixture evenly into the bottom of the prepared baking pan to form the crust. Use the back of a spoon or your fingers to compact it firmly.
4. **Prepare the Raspberry Layer:**
   - If using fresh raspberries, gently mash them with a fork. If using frozen raspberries, thaw and drain them before mashing. Stir in chia seeds if using.
5. **Spread Raspberry Mixture:**
   - Spread the mashed raspberries evenly over the crust layer in the pan.
6. **Bake:**
   - Bake in the preheated oven for 25-30 minutes, or until the edges are golden and the raspberry layer is bubbling.
7. **Cool and Cut:**
   - Allow the bars to cool completely in the pan before transferring to a wire rack to cool completely. Once cooled, cut into squares or bars.
8. **Serve:**
   - Enjoy the bars as a delicious snack or light dessert. They pair well with a cup of tea or coffee.

Tips:

- **Texture:** For a smoother raspberry layer, you can blend the raspberries before spreading them over the crust.
- **Sweetness:** Adjust the sweetness by adding more or less maple syrup or honey, depending on the tartness of your raspberries.

- **Storage:** Store the raspberry coconut bars in an airtight container at room temperature for up to 3 days, or refrigerate for up to 1 week. They can also be frozen for up to 3 months.

Raspberry coconut bars offer a wonderful combination of flavors and textures, making them a delightful and healthy treat. Enjoy making and savoring these tasty bars!

Apple-Pear Crumble

Ingredients:

For the Filling:

- **3 medium apples** (peeled, cored, and sliced; such as Granny Smith or Honeycrisp)
- **3 medium pears** (peeled, cored, and sliced; such as Bartlett or Bosc)
- **1/4 cup granulated sugar** (adjust based on the sweetness of your fruit)
- **1 tablespoon lemon juice**
- **1 tablespoon all-purpose flour** (or cornstarch for a gluten-free option)
- **1 teaspoon ground cinnamon**
- **1/4 teaspoon ground nutmeg** (optional, for extra warmth)
- **1/4 teaspoon salt**

For the Crumble Topping:

- **1/2 cup rolled oats**
- **1/2 cup all-purpose flour** (or a gluten-free flour blend)
- **1/2 cup brown sugar** (packed)
- **1/4 teaspoon ground cinnamon**
- **1/4 teaspoon salt**
- **1/4 cup unsalted butter** (cold, cut into small pieces)

Instructions:

1. **Preheat Oven:**
   - Preheat your oven to 375°F (190°C).
2. **Prepare the Fruit Filling:**
   - In a large bowl, combine the sliced apples and pears with granulated sugar, lemon juice, flour, cinnamon, nutmeg (if using), and salt. Toss until the fruit is evenly coated.
3. **Assemble the Filling:**
   - Transfer the fruit mixture to a greased 9x9-inch baking dish or a similar-sized oven-safe dish. Spread it out evenly.
4. **Prepare the Crumble Topping:**
   - In a separate bowl, mix together the rolled oats, flour, brown sugar, cinnamon, and salt.
   - Cut in the cold butter using a pastry cutter, fork, or your fingers until the mixture resembles coarse crumbs.
5. **Top the Fruit:**
   - Evenly sprinkle the crumble topping over the prepared fruit filling.
6. **Bake:**
   - Bake in the preheated oven for 40-45 minutes, or until the topping is golden brown and the filling is bubbling.

7. **Cool and Serve:**
    - Allow the crumble to cool for a few minutes before serving. This will help the filling set slightly. Serve warm, optionally with a scoop of vanilla ice cream or a dollop of whipped cream.

Tips:

- **Fruit Variety:** Feel free to mix and match different types of apples and pears to suit your taste preferences.
- **Texture:** For a crunchier topping, consider adding some chopped nuts like walnuts or pecans to the crumble mixture.
- **Make Ahead:** The crumble can be assembled ahead of time and stored in the refrigerator for up to 24 hours before baking. Just add a few extra minutes to the baking time if starting from cold.

Apple-pear crumble is a comforting, versatile dessert that's easy to make and perfect for sharing with family and friends. Enjoy this warm, fruity treat!

Strawberry Banana Ice Cream

Ingredients:

- **2 cups fresh or frozen strawberries** (hulled and sliced)
- **2 ripe bananas** (peeled and sliced)
- **1/2 cup coconut milk** (or any milk of your choice; use full-fat for a creamier texture)
- **2 tablespoons honey** or **maple syrup** (optional, for extra sweetness)
- **1 teaspoon vanilla extract** (optional, for added flavor)

Instructions:

1. **Prepare the Fruit:**
   - If using fresh strawberries, hull and slice them. If using frozen strawberries, let them thaw slightly before using.
2. **Blend Ingredients:**
   - In a blender or food processor, combine the strawberries, bananas, and coconut milk. Blend until smooth and creamy.
3. **Sweeten (Optional):**
   - Taste the mixture and add honey or maple syrup if you prefer a sweeter ice cream. Blend again to incorporate the sweetener.
4. **Add Vanilla (Optional):**
   - Stir in vanilla extract if desired for added flavor.
5. **Freeze:**
   - Pour the mixture into an ice cream maker and churn according to the manufacturer's instructions, usually for about 20-25 minutes, until it reaches a soft-serve consistency.
   - If you don't have an ice cream maker, transfer the mixture to a freezer-safe container and freeze for about 2-3 hours, stirring every 30 minutes to prevent ice crystals from forming.
6. **Serve:**
   - Once the ice cream is frozen to your desired consistency, scoop it into bowls or cones and enjoy!
7. **Store:**
   - Store any leftovers in an airtight container in the freezer for up to 1-2 weeks. Allow it to soften for a few minutes at room temperature before scooping.

Tips:

- **Ripeness:** Using very ripe bananas will give your ice cream a natural sweetness and a smoother texture.
- **Texture:** For an ultra-smooth texture, you can blend the mixture a bit longer or add a bit more coconut milk if it's too thick.
- **Flavor Variations:** Feel free to add mix-ins like chocolate chips, nuts, or additional fruits during the last few minutes of churning, or swirl in some fruit puree before freezing.

This strawberry banana ice cream is a healthy and delicious treat that's easy to make and perfect for a hot day or any time you want a sweet, creamy dessert. Enjoy!

Chocolate-Dipped Strawberries

Ingredients:

- **1 pound fresh strawberries** (washed and dried thoroughly; leave the green tops on)
- **8 ounces semi-sweet chocolate** (or your preferred chocolate; use high-quality chocolate for best results)
- **2 tablespoons coconut oil** or **vegetable oil** (optional, for smoother melting and a shinier finish)
- **1/2 cup white chocolate** or **milk chocolate** (optional, for drizzling)

Instructions:

1. **Prepare Strawberries:**
    - Wash the strawberries under cold water and pat them dry completely with paper towels. Any moisture can cause the chocolate to seize, so make sure they are thoroughly dry.
2. **Melt the Chocolate:**
    - **Method 1: Stovetop** – Place the semi-sweet chocolate (and coconut oil, if using) in a heatproof bowl over a pot of simmering water (double boiler). Stir occasionally until melted and smooth.
    - **Method 2: Microwave** – Place the chocolate (and coconut oil, if using) in a microwave-safe bowl. Microwave in 20-second intervals, stirring after each, until completely melted and smooth.
3. **Dip the Strawberries:**
    - Hold each strawberry by the green tops and dip it into the melted chocolate, covering about two-thirds of the berry. Allow any excess chocolate to drip off.
    - Place the dipped strawberries on a parchment-lined baking sheet.
4. **Optional Drizzle:**
    - If using white or milk chocolate for drizzling, melt it as you did with the semi-sweet chocolate.
    - Using a fork or a piping bag, drizzle the melted white or milk chocolate over the dipped strawberries in a decorative pattern.
5. **Chill to Set:**
    - Refrigerate the chocolate-dipped strawberries for at least 30 minutes, or until the chocolate is set and firm.
6. **Serve:**
    - Enjoy the strawberries immediately or store them in the refrigerator for up to 2-3 days.

Tips:

- **Drying:** Ensure the strawberries are completely dry before dipping to prevent the chocolate from separating.
- **Chocolate Quality:** Use good-quality chocolate for the best flavor and texture.

- **Toppings:** Consider rolling the dipped strawberries in crushed nuts, sprinkles, or shredded coconut before the chocolate sets for extra texture and flavor.
- **Storage:** If storing, keep the strawberries in a single layer to prevent them from sticking together. Avoid freezing as it can affect the texture of the strawberries and chocolate.

Chocolate-dipped strawberries are a versatile and delicious treat that can be customized with various types of chocolate and toppings. They make a beautiful addition to any dessert platter or a delightful gift for someone special. Enjoy!

Nutty Fig Bars

Ingredients:

For the Fig Filling:

- **1 cup dried figs** (stems removed, chopped)
- **1/4 cup water** (or more if needed)
- **1 tablespoon honey** or **maple syrup** (optional, for added sweetness)
- **1/2 teaspoon ground cinnamon** (optional, for extra flavor)

For the Nutty Crust:

- **1 cup rolled oats**
- **1/2 cup nuts** (such as almonds, walnuts, or cashews, chopped)
- **1/2 cup almond flour** (or all-purpose flour)
- **1/4 cup coconut oil** (melted, or use unsalted butter)
- **1/4 cup honey** or **maple syrup**
- **1/4 teaspoon salt**

Instructions:

1. **Prepare the Fig Filling:**
   - In a small saucepan, combine the chopped figs and water. Cook over medium heat, stirring occasionally, until the figs are softened and the mixture has thickened, about 5-7 minutes. If needed, add a bit more water to achieve a spreadable consistency.
   - Stir in honey (if using) and ground cinnamon (if using). Remove from heat and let cool.
2. **Prepare the Nutty Crust:**
   - Preheat your oven to 350°F (175°C). Line an 8x8-inch baking pan with parchment paper, leaving a slight overhang for easy removal.
   - In a mixing bowl, combine the rolled oats, chopped nuts, almond flour, melted coconut oil, honey (or maple syrup), and salt. Stir until well mixed and crumbly.
3. **Assemble the Bars:**
   - Press half of the nutty crust mixture into the bottom of the prepared baking pan, packing it down firmly.
   - Spread the fig filling evenly over the crust layer.
   - Sprinkle the remaining nutty crust mixture over the fig filling and press down gently.
4. **Bake:**
   - Bake in the preheated oven for 20-25 minutes, or until the top is golden brown and the edges are crisp.
5. **Cool and Cut:**

- Allow the bars to cool completely in the pan before lifting them out using the parchment paper. Cut into squares or bars.
6. **Serve and Store:**
    - Enjoy the nutty fig bars as a snack or dessert. Store leftovers in an airtight container at room temperature for up to 1 week or refrigerate for longer freshness.

Tips:

- **Texture:** Adjust the texture by blending the fig filling if you prefer a smoother consistency or keep it chunky for more texture.
- **Nuts:** Feel free to use your favorite nuts or a mix of different nuts for variety.
- **Sweetness:** Adjust the sweetness of the fig filling and the crust according to your taste. Some dried figs are sweeter than others, so taste and adjust if needed.

Nutty fig bars are a nutritious and delicious option that combines the natural sweetness of figs with the satisfying crunch of nuts and oats. They're perfect for on-the-go snacking or a healthy treat at any time of the day. Enjoy!

Blueberry Almond Muffins

Ingredients:

For the Muffins:

- **1 1/2 cups all-purpose flour** (or almond flour for a gluten-free option)
- **1/2 cup almond meal** (for added almond flavor)
- **1/2 cup granulated sugar** (or coconut sugar for a healthier option)
- **1/2 cup almond milk** (or any milk of your choice)
- **1/4 cup unsalted butter** (or coconut oil, melted)
- **1/4 cup almond butter** (or any nut butter)
- **2 large eggs**
- **1 teaspoon vanilla extract**
- **1 1/2 teaspoons baking powder**
- **1/2 teaspoon baking soda**
- **1/4 teaspoon salt**
- **1 cup fresh or frozen blueberries** (if using frozen, do not thaw)

For the Topping (optional):

- **2 tablespoons sliced almonds**
- **2 tablespoons sugar** (for sprinkling)

Instructions:

1. **Preheat Oven:**
   - Preheat your oven to 375°F (190°C). Line a 12-cup muffin tin with paper liners or grease the cups.
2. **Mix Dry Ingredients:**
   - In a large bowl, whisk together the all-purpose flour, almond meal, granulated sugar, baking powder, baking soda, and salt.
3. **Mix Wet Ingredients:**
   - In a separate bowl, whisk together the almond milk, melted butter (or coconut oil), almond butter, eggs, and vanilla extract until well combined.
4. **Combine Mixtures:**
   - Add the wet ingredients to the dry ingredients and stir until just combined. Be careful not to overmix; the batter should be slightly lumpy.
   - Gently fold in the blueberries.
5. **Fill Muffin Cups:**
   - Divide the batter evenly among the muffin cups, filling each about 2/3 full.
6. **Add Topping (Optional):**
   - If using, sprinkle the tops of the muffins with sliced almonds and a bit of sugar for added crunch and sweetness.
7. **Bake:**

- Bake in the preheated oven for 18-22 minutes, or until a toothpick inserted into the center of a muffin comes out clean and the tops are golden brown.
8. **Cool and Serve:**
    - Allow the muffins to cool in the pan for 5 minutes, then transfer them to a wire rack to cool completely.
9. **Store:**
    - Store any leftover muffins in an airtight container at room temperature for up to 3 days or freeze for longer storage.

Tips:

- **Blueberries:** If using frozen blueberries, keep them frozen until adding to the batter to prevent them from bleeding into the muffins.
- **Texture:** For a more tender crumb, avoid overmixing the batter. Stir until just combined.
- **Sweetness:** Adjust the amount of sugar based on your preference and the sweetness of your blueberries.

These blueberry almond muffins offer a perfect balance of sweet, nutty, and fruity flavors. They're delicious warm or at room temperature and make a fantastic addition to any meal. Enjoy!

Pineapple Coconut Cake

Ingredients:

For the Cake:

- **1 1/2 cups all-purpose flour**
- **1 cup granulated sugar**
- **1/2 cup unsweetened shredded coconut**
- **1/2 cup unsalted butter** (room temperature)
- **1/2 cup crushed pineapple** (drained, reserving 2 tablespoons of juice)
- **1/2 cup coconut milk** (or any milk of your choice)
- **2 large eggs**
- **1 1/2 teaspoons baking powder**
- **1/2 teaspoon baking soda**
- **1/4 teaspoon salt**
- **1 teaspoon vanilla extract**

For the Frosting:

- **1/2 cup unsalted butter** (room temperature)
- **2 cups powdered sugar**
- **1/4 cup coconut milk** (or more as needed)
- **1/2 cup unsweetened shredded coconut** (toasted, for garnish)
- **1 teaspoon vanilla extract**

Instructions:

1. **Preheat Oven:**
   - Preheat your oven to 350°F (175°C). Grease and flour an 8-inch round cake pan or line it with parchment paper.
2. **Prepare the Cake Batter:**
   - In a medium bowl, whisk together the flour, baking powder, baking soda, and salt.
   - In a large bowl, cream together the butter and granulated sugar until light and fluffy.
   - Beat in the eggs one at a time, then stir in the vanilla extract.
   - Mix in the crushed pineapple and coconut milk until combined.
   - Gradually add the dry ingredients to the wet ingredients, mixing until just combined. Stir in the shredded coconut.
   - Pour the batter into the prepared cake pan and smooth the top with a spatula.
3. **Bake the Cake:**
   - Bake in the preheated oven for 25-30 minutes, or until a toothpick inserted into the center comes out clean and the cake is golden brown.
4. **Cool:**

- Allow the cake to cool in the pan for 10 minutes, then transfer it to a wire rack to cool completely before frosting.
5. **Prepare the Frosting:**
    - In a medium bowl, beat the butter until creamy.
    - Gradually add the powdered sugar, beating until smooth.
    - Mix in the coconut milk and vanilla extract until the frosting reaches your desired consistency. If it's too thick, add a bit more coconut milk; if too thin, add more powdered sugar.
6. **Frost the Cake:**
    - Once the cake is completely cooled, spread the frosting evenly over the top and sides of the cake.
7. **Garnish:**
    - Sprinkle the toasted shredded coconut over the frosted cake for added texture and flavor.
8. **Serve and Store:**
    - Serve the cake at room temperature. Store any leftovers in an airtight container at room temperature for up to 3 days or refrigerate for up to a week.

Tips:

- **Toasting Coconut:** To toast shredded coconut, spread it out on a baking sheet and bake at 350°F (175°C) for 5-7 minutes, stirring occasionally, until golden brown.
- **Pineapple:** Ensure the pineapple is well-drained to avoid excess moisture in the cake batter.
- **Texture:** For a lighter cake, you can use cake flour instead of all-purpose flour.

This pineapple coconut cake is a tropical treat that's sure to impress with its moist texture and delightful flavors. Enjoy making and indulging in this delicious cake!

Peanut Butter Cup Muffins

Ingredients:

For the Muffins:

- 1 1/2 cups all-purpose flour
- 1/2 cup granulated sugar
- 1/4 cup brown sugar (packed)
- 1/2 cup creamy peanut butter
- 1/2 cup milk (any kind)
- 1/4 cup vegetable oil (or melted coconut oil)
- 2 large eggs
- 1 teaspoon vanilla extract
- 1 1/2 teaspoons baking powder
- 1/2 teaspoon baking soda
- 1/4 teaspoon salt
- 1/2 cup mini chocolate chips (or chopped peanut butter cups for added texture)

For the Peanut Butter Cup Swirl (optional):

- 1/2 cup creamy peanut butter (softened)
- 1/4 cup powdered sugar
- 1/4 teaspoon vanilla extract

Instructions:

1. **Preheat Oven:**
   - Preheat your oven to 350°F (175°C). Line a 12-cup muffin tin with paper liners or grease the cups.
2. **Prepare Muffin Batter:**
   - In a large bowl, whisk together the flour, granulated sugar, brown sugar, baking powder, baking soda, and salt.
   - In another bowl, combine the peanut butter, milk, vegetable oil, eggs, and vanilla extract. Mix until smooth and well combined.
   - Add the wet ingredients to the dry ingredients and stir until just combined. Be careful not to overmix.
   - Gently fold in the mini chocolate chips or chopped peanut butter cups.
3. **Prepare Peanut Butter Cup Swirl (Optional):**
   - In a small bowl, mix together the peanut butter, powdered sugar, and vanilla extract until smooth. If it's too thick, you can add a little more milk to achieve a drizzle-able consistency.
4. **Fill Muffin Cups:**
   - Divide the muffin batter evenly among the muffin cups, filling each about 2/3 full.

- If using the peanut butter cup swirl, drop a small spoonful of the peanut butter mixture onto the center of each muffin and use a toothpick or knife to swirl it gently into the batter.
5. **Bake:**
    - Bake in the preheated oven for 18-22 minutes, or until a toothpick inserted into the center comes out clean and the muffins are golden brown.
6. **Cool and Serve:**
    - Allow the muffins to cool in the pan for 5 minutes before transferring them to a wire rack to cool completely.
7. **Store:**
    - Store any leftovers in an airtight container at room temperature for up to 3 days, or refrigerate for up to a week.

Tips:

- **Texture:** For a softer texture, you can use buttermilk or yogurt in place of regular milk.
- **Peanut Butter:** Ensure the peanut butter is creamy and not too oily. Natural peanut butter can be used, but it may affect the texture slightly.
- **Mix-ins:** For extra indulgence, you can fold in additional chopped peanut butter cups or chocolate chips into the batter.

These peanut butter cup muffins are a delicious and satisfying treat that combines the best of chocolate and peanut butter in each bite. Enjoy making and savoring these delightful muffins!

Spiced Pumpkin Energy Balls

Ingredients:

- **1 cup rolled oats**
- **1/2 cup canned pumpkin** (pure pumpkin, not pumpkin pie filling)
- **1/4 cup almond butter** (or peanut butter)
- **1/4 cup honey** or **maple syrup**
- **1/4 cup ground flaxseed** (for added fiber and omega-3s)
- **1/2 teaspoon ground cinnamon**
- **1/4 teaspoon ground nutmeg**
- **1/4 teaspoon ground ginger**
- **1/4 teaspoon ground cloves** (optional, for extra warmth)
- **1/4 cup mini chocolate chips** or **raisins** (optional, for added sweetness and texture)
- **1/4 cup chopped nuts** (optional, for extra crunch)

Instructions:

1. **Combine Ingredients:**
    - In a large bowl, mix together the rolled oats, canned pumpkin, almond butter, honey (or maple syrup), and ground flaxseed.
2. **Add Spices:**
    - Stir in the ground cinnamon, nutmeg, ginger, and cloves (if using) until the mixture is well combined.
3. **Mix in Extras:**
    - If desired, fold in the mini chocolate chips, raisins, and/or chopped nuts.
4. **Form the Balls:**
    - Using your hands or a small cookie scoop, form the mixture into bite-sized balls, about 1 inch in diameter. If the mixture is too sticky, lightly dampen your hands with water to help shape the balls.
5. **Chill:**
    - Place the energy balls on a parchment-lined baking sheet or plate and refrigerate for at least 30 minutes to firm up.
6. **Store:**
    - Store the spiced pumpkin energy balls in an airtight container in the refrigerator for up to 1 week, or freeze for up to 3 months.

Tips:

- **Texture:** If the mixture is too dry, add a bit more almond butter or honey. If too wet, add a few more oats or flaxseed.
- **Spices:** Adjust the spices to your taste. Feel free to experiment with other spices like cardamom or allspice.
- **Add-Ins:** Customize your energy balls with different add-ins like dried cranberries, coconut flakes, or chia seeds.

These spiced pumpkin energy balls are a perfect combination of convenience and flavor, offering a healthy snack that's both satisfying and easy to prepare. Enjoy these tasty treats any time you need a quick pick-me-up!

Gingerbread Date Bars

Ingredients:

For the Bars:

- **1 cup pitted dates** (soaked in warm water for 10 minutes, then drained)
- **1 cup old-fashioned rolled oats**
- **1/2 cup almond flour** (or all-purpose flour)
- **1/2 cup chopped nuts** (such as almonds, walnuts, or pecans)
- **1/4 cup molasses** (for that classic gingerbread flavor)
- **1/4 cup coconut oil** (melted, or use unsalted butter)
- **1 teaspoon ground ginger**
- **1 teaspoon ground cinnamon**
- **1/4 teaspoon ground cloves**
- **1/4 teaspoon ground nutmeg**
- **1/4 teaspoon salt**

For the Glaze (optional):

- **1/2 cup powdered sugar**
- **1-2 tablespoons milk** (or any milk substitute)
- **1/4 teaspoon vanilla extract**

Instructions:

1. **Preheat Oven:**
    - Preheat your oven to 350°F (175°C). Line an 8x8-inch baking pan with parchment paper, leaving a slight overhang for easy removal.
2. **Prepare the Date Mixture:**
    - In a food processor, combine the pitted dates and process until they form a smooth paste. If the dates are too sticky, you can add a little water, a teaspoon at a time, until you get a smooth consistency.
3. **Combine Dry Ingredients:**
    - In a large mixing bowl, combine the rolled oats, almond flour, chopped nuts, ground ginger, ground cinnamon, ground cloves, ground nutmeg, and salt.
4. **Mix Wet Ingredients:**
    - In a separate bowl, mix together the date paste, molasses, and melted coconut oil until well combined.
5. **Combine and Mix:**
    - Add the wet ingredients to the dry ingredients and stir until fully combined. The mixture should be thick and slightly crumbly.
6. **Press Into Pan:**
    - Press the mixture evenly into the prepared baking pan, packing it down firmly with the back of a spoon or a spatula.

7. **Bake:**
   - Bake in the preheated oven for 20-25 minutes, or until the edges are golden brown and the bars are set.
8. **Cool and Cut:**
   - Allow the bars to cool in the pan for 10 minutes, then lift them out using the parchment paper. Let them cool completely on a wire rack before cutting into squares or bars.
9. **Prepare Glaze (Optional):**
   - If using, whisk together the powdered sugar, milk, and vanilla extract until smooth. Drizzle the glaze over the cooled bars.
10. **Serve and Store:**
    - Enjoy the gingerbread date bars as a tasty snack or dessert. Store them in an airtight container at room temperature for up to 1 week, or refrigerate for longer freshness.

Tips:

- **Dates:** Ensure the dates are soft and moist for easy processing. If they're too dry, soak them longer or add a little water.
- **Flavors:** Adjust the spices according to your taste preferences. You can also add a bit of orange zest or dried fruit for extra flavor.
- **Texture:** For a chunkier texture, chop the dates and nuts before adding them to the mixture.

These gingerbread date bars are a wonderful way to enjoy the warm spices of gingerbread in a nutritious, easy-to-make snack. Enjoy making and indulging in these delicious bars!

Frozen Yogurt Bark

Ingredients:

For the Base:

- **2 cups plain Greek yogurt** (or any flavor you prefer)
- **2 tablespoons honey** or **maple syrup** (adjust to taste for sweetness)
- **1 teaspoon vanilla extract** (optional)

For the Toppings:

- **1/2 cup fresh berries** (such as strawberries, blueberries, raspberries, or blackberries)
- **1/4 cup granola**
- **1/4 cup chopped nuts** (such as almonds, walnuts, or pecans)
- **1/4 cup shredded coconut**
- **1/4 cup mini chocolate chips** or **cacao nibs** (optional)
- **1 tablespoon chia seeds** (optional, for added nutrition)

Instructions:

1. **Prepare the Yogurt Base:**
    - In a bowl, mix together the Greek yogurt, honey (or maple syrup), and vanilla extract until well combined.
2. **Prepare Baking Sheet:**
    - Line a baking sheet with parchment paper or a silicone baking mat. This will make it easier to remove the frozen yogurt bark later.
3. **Spread Yogurt:**
    - Spread the yogurt mixture evenly onto the prepared baking sheet. Use a spatula to smooth it out to about 1/4 inch thick. The thickness can be adjusted to your preference.
4. **Add Toppings:**
    - Evenly sprinkle the fresh berries, granola, chopped nuts, shredded coconut, mini chocolate chips (or cacao nibs), and chia seeds over the yogurt base. Press the toppings lightly into the yogurt to ensure they stick.
5. **Freeze:**
    - Place the baking sheet in the freezer and freeze for at least 2 hours, or until the yogurt is completely frozen and firm.
6. **Break into Pieces:**
    - Once frozen, break the yogurt bark into pieces. You can use your hands or a knife to break it into desired sizes.
7. **Serve and Store:**
    - Serve the frozen yogurt bark immediately or store the pieces in an airtight container in the freezer. It's best enjoyed straight from the freezer, as it will soften if left out at room temperature.

Tips:

- **Yogurt:** Use full-fat Greek yogurt for a creamier texture, or opt for non-fat or low-fat versions if you prefer.
- **Toppings:** Feel free to get creative with toppings. Other great options include dried fruit, crushed nuts, seeds, or even a drizzle of nut butter.
- **Sweetness:** Adjust the amount of honey or maple syrup based on your taste and the sweetness of your yogurt.

Frozen yogurt bark is a versatile and delicious treat that you can customize with your favorite toppings. It's a great way to enjoy a healthy snack while indulging in a bit of sweetness. Enjoy making and snacking on this delightful treat!

Coconut Raspberry Muffins

Ingredients:

For the Muffins:

- **1 1/2 cups all-purpose flour**
- **1/2 cup shredded coconut** (unsweetened or sweetened, based on your preference)
- **1/2 cup granulated sugar** (or coconut sugar for a less refined option)
- **1/4 cup coconut oil** (melted, or use unsalted butter)
- **1/2 cup coconut milk** (or any milk of your choice)
- **1/4 cup plain Greek yogurt** (or buttermilk)
- **2 large eggs**
- **1 teaspoon vanilla extract**
- **1 1/2 teaspoons baking powder**
- **1/2 teaspoon baking soda**
- **1/4 teaspoon salt**
- **1 cup fresh raspberries** (or frozen raspberries, thawed and drained)

For the Topping (optional):

- **2 tablespoons shredded coconut** (for sprinkling)
- **2 tablespoons granulated sugar** (for sprinkling)

Instructions:

1. **Preheat Oven:**
    - Preheat your oven to 350°F (175°C). Line a 12-cup muffin tin with paper liners or grease the cups.
2. **Prepare Dry Ingredients:**
    - In a large bowl, whisk together the flour, shredded coconut, granulated sugar, baking powder, baking soda, and salt.
3. **Mix Wet Ingredients:**
    - In another bowl, whisk together the melted coconut oil, coconut milk, Greek yogurt, eggs, and vanilla extract until well combined.
4. **Combine Mixtures:**
    - Add the wet ingredients to the dry ingredients and stir until just combined. Be careful not to overmix; the batter should be slightly lumpy.
5. **Fold in Raspberries:**
    - Gently fold the raspberries into the batter. If using frozen raspberries, fold them in carefully to prevent the batter from turning pink.
6. **Fill Muffin Cups:**
    - Divide the batter evenly among the muffin cups, filling each about 2/3 full.
7. **Add Topping (Optional):**

- If desired, sprinkle the tops of the muffins with additional shredded coconut and granulated sugar for a sweet, crunchy topping.

8. **Bake:**
   - Bake in the preheated oven for 18-22 minutes, or until a toothpick inserted into the center of a muffin comes out clean and the tops are golden brown.
9. **Cool:**
   - Allow the muffins to cool in the pan for 5 minutes, then transfer them to a wire rack to cool completely.
10. **Store:**
    - Store any leftover muffins in an airtight container at room temperature for up to 3 days, or refrigerate for up to a week.

Tips:

- **Raspberries:** If using frozen raspberries, do not thaw them before adding to the batter to avoid bleeding. Gently fold them in to prevent color transfer.
- **Coconut:** Adjust the amount of shredded coconut based on your preference for coconut flavor and texture.
- **Texture:** For extra moist muffins, consider adding a tablespoon of chia seeds or flaxseeds to the batter.

These coconut raspberry muffins are a perfect combination of sweet and nutty with a burst of fresh fruit. Enjoy these delicious muffins as a treat any time of day!

Chocolate Chia Seed Pudding

Ingredients:

- **1/2 cup chia seeds**
- **2 cups almond milk** (or any milk of your choice, such as coconut milk, oat milk, or dairy milk)
- **1/4 cup unsweetened cocoa powder**
- **1/4 cup pure maple syrup** or **honey** (adjust to taste)
- **1 teaspoon vanilla extract**
- **A pinch of salt**

Optional Toppings:

- **Fresh berries** (such as strawberries, raspberries, or blueberries)
- **Sliced banana**
- **Shredded coconut**
- **Chopped nuts** (such as almonds, walnuts, or pecans)
- **Mini chocolate chips** or **cacao nibs**

Instructions:

1. **Combine Ingredients:**
   - In a large bowl or a mixing jar with a lid, whisk together the chia seeds, almond milk, cocoa powder, maple syrup (or honey), vanilla extract, and a pinch of salt until well combined.
2. **Mix Well:**
   - Allow the mixture to sit for about 5 minutes, then whisk again to break up any clumps of chia seeds. This helps to ensure an even texture.
3. **Chill:**
   - Cover the bowl or jar and refrigerate for at least 4 hours, or overnight. The chia seeds will absorb the liquid and swell, creating a thick, pudding-like texture.
4. **Stir Before Serving:**
   - Before serving, give the pudding a good stir to ensure a smooth consistency. If the pudding is too thick, you can stir in a little more milk to reach your desired consistency.
5. **Add Toppings:**
   - Spoon the pudding into bowls or glasses and add your favorite toppings, such as fresh berries, sliced banana, shredded coconut, chopped nuts, or mini chocolate chips.
6. **Serve:**
   - Enjoy the chocolate chia seed pudding immediately, or keep it in the refrigerator for up to 5 days.

Tips:

- **Sweetness:** Adjust the amount of maple syrup or honey based on your preference for sweetness. You can also use other sweeteners like agave syrup or stevia if desired.
- **Cocoa Powder:** Use high-quality unsweetened cocoa powder for the best chocolate flavor.
- **Consistency:** For a creamier pudding, you can blend the mixture after chilling to smooth out any remaining clumps of chia seeds.

This chocolate chia seed pudding is a versatile and healthy treat that's perfect for satisfying your chocolate cravings while keeping things nutritious. Enjoy this easy and delicious pudding as a quick snack or a decadent dessert!

www.ingramcontent.com/pod-product-compliance
Lightning Source LLC
LaVergne TN
LVHW081605060526
838201LV00054B/2083